T0210615

Web Data APIs
for Knowledge Graphs

Easing Access to Semantic Data

for Application Developers

Synthesis Lectures on Data, Semantics, and Knowledge

Editor

Ying Ding, *University of Texas at Austin*
Paul Groth, *University of Amsterdam*

Founding Editor Emeritus
James Hendler, *Rensselaer Polytechnic Institute*

Synthesis Lectures on Data, Semantics, and Knowledge is edited by Ying Ding of the University of Texas at Austin and Paul Groth of the University of Amsterdam. The series focuses on the pivotal role that data on the web and the emergent technologies that surround it play both in the evolution of the World Wide Web as well as applications in domains requiring data integration and semantic analysis. The large-scale availability of both structured and unstructured data on the Web has enabled radically new technologies to develop. It has impacted developments in a variety of areas including machine learning, deep learning, semantic search, and natural language processing. Knowledge and semantics are a critical foundation for the sharing, utilization, and organization of this data. The series aims both to provide pathways into the field of research and an understanding of the principles underlying these technologies for an audience of scientists, engineers, and practitioners.
Topics to be included:

- Knowledge graphs, both public and private

- Linked Data

- Knowledge graph and automated knowledge base construction

- Knowledge engineering for large-scale data

- Machine reading

- Uses of Semantic Web technologies

- Information and knowledge integration, data fusion

- Various forms of semantics on the web (e.g., ontologies, language models, and distributional semantics)

- Terminology, Thesaurus, & Ontology Management

- Query languages

Social Semantic Web Mining
Tope Omitola, Sebastián A. Ríos, and John G. Breslin
2015

Semantic Breakthrough in Drug Discovery
Bin Chen, Huijun Wang, Ying Ding, and David Wild
2014

Semantics in Mobile Sensing
Zhixian Yan and Dipanjan Chakraborty
2014

Provenance: An Introduction to PROV
Luc Moreau and Paul Groth
2013

Resource-Oriented Architecture Patterns for Webs of Data
Brian Sletten
2013

Aaron Swartz's A Programmable Web: An Unfinished Work
Aaron Swartz
2013

Incentive-Centric Semantic Web Application Engineering
Elena Simperl, Roberta Cuel, and Martin Stein
2013

Publishing and Using Cultural Heritage Linked Data on the Semantic Web
Eero Hyvönen
2012

VIVO: A Semantic Approach to Scholarly Networking and Discovery
Katy Börner, Michael Conlon, Jon Corson-Rikert, and Ying Ding
2012

Linked Data: Evolving the Web into a Global Data Space
Tom Heath and Christian Bizer
2011

Web Data APIs for Knowledge Graphs: Easing Access to Semantic Data for Application Developers
Albert Meroño-Peñuela, Pasquale Lisena, and Carlos Martínez-Ortiz

ISBN: 978-3-031-00789-7   paperback
ISBN: 978-3-031-01917-3   ebook
ISBN: 978-3-031-00112-3   hardcover

DOI 10.1007/978-3-031-01917-3

A Publication in the Springer series
SYNTHESIS LECTURES ON DATA, SEMANTICS, AND KNOWLEDGE

Lecture #21
Series Editors: Ying Ding, *University of Texas at Austin*
                Paul Groth, *University of Amsterdam*
Founding Editor Emeritus: James Hendler, *Rensselaer Polytechnic Institute*
Series ISSN
Print 2691-2023   Electronic 2691-2031

Web Data APIs
for Knowledge Graphs

Easing Access to Semantic Data

for Application Developers

Albert Meroño-Peñuela
King's College London, United Kingdom

Pasquale Lisena
EURECOM, France

Carlos Martínez-Ortiz
Netherlands eScience Center, The Netherlands

SYNTHESIS LECTURES ON DATA, SEMANTICS, AND KNOWLEDGE #21

ABSTRACT

This book describes a set of methods, architectures, and tools to extend the data pipeline at the disposal of developers when they need to publish and consume data from Knowledge Graphs (graph-structured knowledge bases that describe the entities and relations within a domain in a semantically meaningful way) using SPARQL, Web APIs, and JSON. To do so, it focuses on the paradigmatic cases of two middleware software packages, *grlc* and *SPARQL Transformer*, which automatically build and run SPARQL-based REST APIs and allow the specification of JSON schema results, respectively. The authors highlight the underlying principles behind these technologies—query management, declarative languages, new levels of indirection, abstraction layers, and separation of concerns—, explain their practical usage, and describe their penetration in research projects and industry. The book, therefore, serves a double purpose: to provide a sound and technical description of tools and methods at the disposal of publishers and developers to quickly deploy and consume Web Data APIs on top of Knowledge Graphs; and to propose an extensible and heterogeneous Knowledge Graph access infrastructure that accommodates a growing ecosystem of querying paradigms.

KEYWORDS

knowledge graphs, web APIs, querying infrastructures, query interfaces, SPARQL, *grlc*

Contents

Foreword

Knowledge Graphs have recently emerged as a powerful concept and highly valuable technology. They can also be seen as the third umbrella term of the line of research and practice that started from the vision called the Semantic Web, which in some fields later became more commonly known under the name of Linked Data and is now often labeled Knowledge Graphs. These different umbrellas have much of the underlying concepts and technologies in common, but also come with clear differences in focus. Openness and decentralization are aspects that have shifted out of focus with the rise of the third umbrella term. Knowledge Graphs are often associated with big companies unilaterally building silo-like databases, with no particular emphasis on making this knowledge accessible to third parties or on keeping the architecture decentralized. Recently, however, I see that an increasing number of fields and communities are embracing the term Knowledge Graph for smaller and more restricted knowledge bases, and they are also pushing openness and decentralization back into focus. They also often promote the use of the core Semantic Web language RDF, which the big companies were hesitant to adopt. Web Data APIs have, in my view, an important role in this development because they lower the bar for interoperability and reuse. While the problems of interoperability and reuse have received a large amount of theoretical consideration, ever since the inception of the Semantic Web vision, they have been lacking in practical solutions for many scenarios. In a constructive and incremental way, Web Data APIs have started to fill in the last missing gaps to make Knowledge Graphs work as ecosystems rather than just systems. Web Data APIs enable small and large knowledge bases to connect and build upon each other, and they thereby form a crucial component in this development.

The query language SPARQL has been a core technological component for a large portion of the approaches under the umbrella terms introduced above. SPARQL can be seen as a success story, with its high adoption rate and the availability of countless implementations and related tools. SPARQL can, however, also be seen as a problem child. It is known to be hard to use by developers who have not received specific training, and even experienced users like myself often depend on copy–paste templates as a starting point. On the server side, moreover, SPARQL endpoints are notoriously difficult to set up in a way they can reliably and efficiently answer all the possible queries they are supposed to be able to handle. In my opinion, Web Data APIs are underway to solve these problems, not by replacing SPARQL but by building upon it and only slightly redrawing its architectural role. That is exactly what the authors of this book did by developing *grlc* and *SPARQL Transformer*, the two core components described in this book. With just a few lines of declarative code, a SPARQL query template is turned into a developer-friendly Web Data API.

I therefore believe that this book is a must-read for everybody involved in the engineering parts of Knowledge Graph projects that build upon the RDF technology. Moreover, it might convince you to choose RDF technology in the first place. Most of the downsides of RDF you might have heard about are eliminated with the methods and tools described in this book, while its strengths are in full force. With these strengths, the knowledge in your Knowledge Graph can get a life of its own and can become part of the higher realm of our shared human knowledge.

Tobias Kuhn
June 2021

Preface

Knowledge Graphs are among the most exciting and disruptive technological developments of our time. Heavily inspired by ideas from the Semantic Web and Linked Data communities, Knowledge Graphs are graph-structured knowledge bases that describe the entities and relations in a domain in a semantically meaningful way. This is typically done through the data model and syntax provided by the Resource Description Framework (RDF) [Cyganiak et al., 2014], a Web data publishing paradigm based on structured statements of subject-predicate-object triples suitable for machine consumption. For example, Wikidata [Vrandečić and Krötzsch, 2014], a Knowledge Graph built collaboratively by more than 20,000 volunteers, describes more than 90 million items for anyone to reuse under a CC0 public domain license. The concepts and relationships thus described in Knowledge Graphs are frequently used in intelligent systems like Google Search (visible in the knowledge panels of its results page), Siri, and Alexa (through voice-assisted answers), and provide these systems with some degree of understanding of the world.

But how can we use the wealth of knowledge contained in Knowledge Graphs in *our* applications? Is this some intricate mechanism that only large tech corporations like Google, Apple, and Amazon can afford? Or, on the contrary, **can *any* developer query these Knowledge Graphs?**

The answer to this question is far from being trivial, and the main objective of this book is providing an accurate one. A first version of this answer, known to experienced Knowledge Graph developers, is a firm *yes*, backed by the existence of standard, declarative, and rich query languages that can be used to interrogate these Knowledge Graphs from applications and get back results. The SPARQL Protocol and Query Language [W3C SPARQL working group, 2013], for example, is one of these languages. SPARQL operates over HTTP, the same protocol developers use to transfer Web pages and Web API data responses from servers to clients, and therefore it is easy to see how it can be used to transfer Knowledge Graph data on the Web and will remain a fine mechanism to do so for a great variety of users. Moreover, clients of SPARQL-compliant servers can always request results of their queries to be returned in JSON [Bourhis et al., 2017], the *de facto* Web API data transfer format, thus making it in principle friendly to the technology stack developers are used to.

Why, then, this book? Aren't RDF, SPARQL,[1] and JSON enough to query Knowledge Graphs? In our view, there are at least four reasons these technologies do not cut it for *any* developer who wishes to query RDF Knowledge Graphs—especially if that developer is used to other querying paradigms.

1. The first reason is that, although this is a somewhat uncomfortable truth, SPARQL is an uncommon query language among developers: only a tiny fraction of developers know—or are keen to learn—how to handle RDF data or write SPARQL queries [Booth et al., 2019]. The immense ma-

---

[1] We use here SPARQL as a prototypical example, and we intend to illustrate the situation for all Knowledge Graph query languages, not just SPARQL. We do not mean to criticize SPARQL in particular; we are, as we will see later in the book, quite fond of SPARQL.

jority of Web developers are used to query data published under the *de facto* standard paradigm of Web APIs. Are these two, SPARQL and Web APIs, confronted paradigms in querying Knowledge Graphs? Or can we devise ways of combining their strengths?

2. The second reason is that writing SPARQL queries from within application code can get very repetitive. Large applications need huge amounts of data, leading to lots of queries that developers need to type over and over again. Is there a way to reuse, somehow, these queries, and avoid redundant labor?

3. This leads to the third reason: query management. In general, dealing with SPARQL queries—or any Knowledge Graph queries for that matter—inside application code is more often based on craftsmanship and improvisation rather than on principled and systematic engineering. Queries end up hard-coded and mixed with application source code, poorly documented and spread in several separate files, at best. What should better query management look like?

4. A fourth reason limiting SPARQL is its inability to let developers indicate *how* they would like their query results to be structured. SPARQL is extraordinarily effective in letting developers specify *what* to query in a declarative way. However, is rather limited in *how* these results are returned, typically in a table-like form even when data is requested in the richly structured JSON format. In fact, JSON-LD—the RDF serialization proposed for the use in Web-based environments [Sporny et al., 2013]—is not among the possible output formats of a SELECT query. Developers need—and are therefore forced—to manipulate and appropriately shape the structure of JSON results themselves in a post-hoc manner. How can we extend the available standards to allow and generalize precisely that?

These are important concerns that many developers often find themselves confronted with in production environments. In this book, we describe a set of methods, architectures, and tools to overcome these limitations, and we extend the data pipeline at the disposal of developers when they need to publish and consume data from Knowledge Graphs with SPARQL, Web APIs, and JSON. To do so, we focus on the paradigmatic cases of two middleware software packages that we wrote, and currently maintain: *grlc* [Meroño-Peñuela and Hoekstra, 2016, 2017] and *SPARQL Transformer* [Lisena et al., 2019]. Both *grlc* and *SPARQL Transformer* have reached maturity and wide community use, and we believe are useful tools to tackle these challenges. They are, respectively, targeted at automatically generating SPARQL-based Web APIs for Knowledge Graphs and at allowing developers to specify the shape in which they desire to receive their SPARQL JSON results.

The blooming ecosystem of solutions, models, and ideas around Knowledge Graphs challenge our classic conceptions about how to represent, store, and share data, but it also comes with an overwhelming variety of technologies and standards. Therefore, deciding *what* specific technologies belong to the "Knowledge Graph technology stack" is a difficult challenge with many different answers, which will depend on specific developer goals. We are choosing what these "Knowledge Graph technologies" are by looking at you, the reader, and imagining you as an application developer who is interested in querying or otherwise building a Web application or API over a Knowledge Graph. Part of the premise of the book is that you want to do this by leveraging as much data as possible, in particular existing large repositories of *Linked Data*: a Web data publishing paradigm that relies on HTTP, RDF, and SPARQL under which billions of unique statements over hundreds of thousands of datasets and domains [Fernández et al., 2017, Heath and Bizer, 2011] have been published in the last two decades. This means that knowledge of RDF, SPARQL, and Linked Data is required to fully appreciate the book, and that by being an application developer you might not be an expert on those topics just yet. In order to address this, we start the book with a short introduction to these subjects, and we point you to additional materials that we think are valuable teaching resources that will quickly get you on track. If you are new to the Linked Data, RDF, and SPARQL world, we strongly encourage you to read on and familiarize yourself with these topics before you proceed to the remainder of the book. If you are a developer who already knows about RDF and SPARQL, that's great! Please feel free to skip Chapter 1 altogether. You can also quickly skim through it and use it as a recap. If, on the other hand, you are an application developer who has *never* built or dealt with Web APIs, we also have got you covered with an introduction to that in Chapter 3.

We have written this book with the idea of transcending a mere technical manual about these tools, and consequently emphasize the *principles* behind our design choices rather than the tools themselves. Some of these principles are:

- query management: distributed query storage and publishing over decentralized systems;

- declarative languages: mapping API specifications to SPARQL; mapping SPARQL output to arbitrarily structured JSON;

- new levels of indirection: globally and uniquely identifying queries on the Web; and

- Knowledge Graph access: multi-tier architectures, separation of concerns.

We will refer to these principles across the book as we resort to them through the chapters. The book is, therefore, organized as follows.

- **Chapter 1** is a quick introduction to the background required for the book, and introduces the core ideas behind Linked Data, RDF, and SPARQL as the basic technology stack for building and querying Knowledge Graphs and representing semantic data on the Web. We also outline other relevant technologies for Knowledge Graphs, such as GraphQL.

- **Chapter 2** describes how to access Knowledge Graphs programmatically. We explain the underlying principles of HTTP and SPARQL, the main protocols involved in querying Knowledge Graphs, and how to use them within application code, with various examples. We then show how several libraries can accelerate this process under two assumptions: (1) that developers just want to execute some SPARQL remotely and use the results and (2) that developers want to manipulate output from SPARQL.

- **Chapter 3** is about how to build Web data APIs on top of SPARQL. Here, we dive deeper into the main paradigmatic differences between SPARQL and Web APIs, as the two confronted models of Web data querying we are interested in for this book. We explain the entire bottom-up process of building such APIs on top of SPARQL by explaining the OpenAPI specification (the *de facto* standard), how to merge it with SPARQL, and the consequences of doing so manually.

- **Chapter 4** revolves around automating the processes explained in Chapter 3 through sharing queries with *grlc*. We explain its underlying principles, and we describe a lightweight query documentation and metadata language to map features of the OpenAPI specification to SPARQL. We include here some exercises for training on the explained content.

- **Chapter 5** explains how to shape the JSON results of SPARQL queries, addressing another important process of the Knowledge Graph data consumption pipeline of Chapter 3. We explain what the curse of the bindings is, and how to use a single JSON object as both query and results template in *SPARQL Transformer*. We also describe its architecture, features, and syntax, and how to integrate it with *grlc*. Again, we include some exercises.

- **Chapter 6** collects a number of successful uses and applications of the tools and principles presented in previous chapters. We provide abundant documentation and links to resources.

- **Chapter 7** presents our conclusions and future challenges, answering some of the questions pointed out in this introduction.

We have created a series of exercises at the end of Chapters 4 and 5 to practice the core knowledge introduced in them. You will find their solutions in an appendix at the end of the book, so you can study them comfortably without having the solutions too temptingly close. Please, only look at them once you have tried to solve the exercises by yourself. For your convenience, we have also uploaded these exercises and their solutions, together with all code snippets used in the book, to an online repository[2] where they are easier to use in practical settings. In addition, you will find there the materials and slides that we used for the *SPARQL Endpoints and Web API* (**SWApi**) tutorials that we organized during the International Semantic Web Conference 2020 (ISWC 2020), the Web Conference 2021 (TheWebConf 2021), and the Extended Semantic Web Conference 2021 (ESWC 2021). The book that you are about to start is based on those tutorials: it provides a more fluid narrative around Web APIs for RDF Knowledge Graphs and adds a substantial amount of references, exercises, and background knowledge in order to make its contents more accessible to a wider range of Web developers.

---

[2]https://github.com/api4kg

We hope that you enjoy reading the book as much as we have enjoyed writing it. We will consider our efforts a big success if we made your life as a developer a little easier, or if we inspired you to make your own ideas around APIs and Knowledge Graphs grow. Have lots of fun!

Albert Meroño-Peñuela, Pasquale Lisena, and Carlos Martínez-Ortiz
July 2021

Acknowledgments

The idea of this book came from a series of tutorials that we organized in academic conferences around the Semantic Web and Knowledge Graphs, concretely at the International Semantic Web Conference 2020 (ISWC 2020), the Web Conference 2021 (TheWebConf 2021), and the Extended Semantic Web Conference 2021 (ESWC 2021). Initially, the plan was just to extend and solidify the contents of those tutorials into a more permanent format, but we soon realized that, on top of that, we also wanted to expand our audiences and talk not just to the amazing community of Semantic Web developers, but also to Web developers with a passion for data and knowledge in general. Executing this plan, which would result in the writing of this book, required much more than just our own hands.

First, and foremost, we would like to thank our series editors, Paul Groth and Ying Ding, for offering us the opportunity to publish our book with them, and especially to Paul for the idea of turning our tutorial into a book. We are very grateful to Michael Morgan at Morgan & Claypool for his brilliant and effective guidance through the editing process. Thanks also to Christine Kiilerich for her essential help on editing. Very special thanks to Aidan Hogan for reviewing the book, and his essential suggestions for increasing its quality and reach to wider audiences.

We will always be grateful to the Semantic Web and eScience academic communities for their vibrant support and constructive criticism. Among them, we want to thank our mentors who have always inspired and motivated us to pursue and refine our ideas. Thanks to Rinke Hoekstra for saying "just write your own implementation," hence proving that good ideas come not only from good papers, but also from good code. Thank you to Frank van Harmelen for being a true beacon of science and supporting our research adventures even when the outcomes were not that clear, and to Richard Zijdeman, for giving us freedom way beyond the budget, being our best ambassador and tester, and the true realization of interdisciplinary research. Thank you to Raphaël Troncy, who has been a great supporter and sponsor, encouraging throughout the writing of this book and the development of some of the technologies presented here. Thanks to our dear friend Ilaria Tiddi, who put us in contact for the first time; without her, our collaboration (and this book) may not have been possible. In addition, very special thanks go to our esteemed colleagues and friends. Finally, a big, big thank you to Tobias Kuhn for being an enthusiastic user, an exceptional researcher, and for writing the foreword of this book.

We owe a well-deserved acknowledgment to all the institutions that have supported the research contained in this book. We would like to thank the Netherlands eScience Center for their continued support to *grlc* over the years and in the preparation of this book. We are deeply grateful to CLARIAH, CLARIAH NL, and CLARIAH-PLUS, and to Henk Wals, Kees Mandemakers, Frank van Harmelen, Jan Luiten van Zanden, Richard Zijdeman, and Auke Rijpma for supporting and funding the research that led to this book.

Finally, our deepest gratitude goes to you, the developers, for carrying out the work that keeps the world connected through the Web. Thank you to all the *grlc* and *SPARQL Transformer* contributors for your code, your issues, and your wisdom, with special thanks to Rinke Hoekstra, Richard Zijdeman, Roderick van der Weerdt, Jaap Blom, Arnold Kuzniar, Mari Wigham, Jurriaan Spaaks, Jonas Jetschni, and Ruud Steltenpool. Thanks to John Walker for his enthusiastic support and reporting key issues. A big thank you to the SALAD (Services and Applications over Linked APIs and Data) community, the community of Semantic Web developers, and Web developers from all walks of life. It is for you that we have written this book. We hope you enjoy it!

Albert Meroño-Peñuela, Pasquale Lisena, and Carlos Martínez-Ortiz
July 2021

CHAPTER 1

Knowledge Graphs of Linked Data

This first chapter introduces the concepts of Knowledge Graphs and Linked Data, and the technical specifications of RDF, and SPARQL as paradigmatic implementations of these concepts. These technologies have gained a lot of traction in recent years in both academia and industry, as shown by large Knowledge Graphs like Wikidata and DBpedia, and those fueling the services of Google, Microsoft, Apple, Facebook, Amazon, Yahoo, and LinkedIn. Writing an exhaustive chapter—which would easily turn into a book, see, e.g., [Hogan et al., 2021]—about all the technologies involved in the construction and access of these Knowledge Graphs is out of the scope of this book. Instead, we focus on a specific view of what Knowledge Graphs are: a data representation paradigm that uses graphs of *linked data* to represent knowledge through a set of W3C Web standards.[1] This is, however, just a pragmatic decision: Knowledge Graphs are not one single, unanimously recognized technology stack. In fact, there are many interesting, alternative ways of implementing Knowledge Graphs outside the space of Linked Data, for example, through *property graphs* which are becoming increasingly popular in various domains. In order to give a flavor of these alternatives, we also provide a brief introduction to GraphQL at the end of the chapter.

Therefore, this chapter is really meant to provide the necessary knowledge on RDF, SPARQL and JSON that will be needed for the remainder of the book, rather than being a complete introduction to all technologies and ideas around Knowledge Graphs. Since this is a space where a lot of novel ideas are developing quickly, we will provide, at the end of each section, a list of references and external resources for readers interested in learning more about these subjects (although reading those is not required to advance in the book). Developers who are experienced in deploying Semantic Web and Linked Data applications can safely skip this chapter and continue to Chapter 2.

1.1 KNOWLEDGE GRAPHS AND LINKED DATA

Knowledge Graphs are built upon "the core idea of using graphs to represent data, often enhanced with some way to explicitly represent knowledge" in "application scenarios that involve integrating, managing and extracting value from diverse sources of data at large scale" [Hogan et al., 2021]. References to these ideas, and to the term itself, can be traced back to the 1950s, 1960s, and 1970s [Gutierrez and Sequeda, 2020], and were coined around the general idea of *semantic networks* and the data structures that could support rich descriptions of domains that were needed for the research

---
[1]See https://www.w3.org/standards/semanticweb/data.

being developed at the time around knowledge representation and reasoning. However, in 2012 Google popularized the term when it released the Google Knowledge Graph [Blog, 2012] to support the generation of its now famous knowledge panels in Web searches; many other Knowledge Graphs followed to the extent that no list can account for how many of them are out there anymore.

But before this happened, the Semantic Web community had been using the term *Linked Data* since at least 2006[2] to refer to a concept with many overlaps with Knowledge Graphs. Similar to the Web of HTML documents, Linked Data proposes four basic principles to interconnect data bits on the Web

1. use URIs as names for things;

2. use HTTP URIs so that people can look up those names;

3. when someone looks up a URI, provide useful information, using the standards (RDF, SPARQL); and

4. include links to other URIs so that they can discover more things.

In this way, a "graph" of connected URIs can be published (with RDF statements; see Section 1.2), queried (with SPARQL; see Section 1.3), and traversed (with HTTP; see Chapter 2) just as we usually do with Web HTML documents; this time, however, machines can process the knowledge made explicit in the graph—contrarily to HTML documents containing human language, which needs a great deal of Natural Language Processing (NLP). These principles, together with standards like Linked Data Platform (LDP) [Speicher et al., 2015] and initiatives for vocabulary reuse such as *schema.org* [Guha et al., 2016] and Linked Open Vocabularies [Vandenbussche et al., 2017], made an entire ecosystem of hundreds of thousands of Linked Data datasets available to the public with billions of triples [Fernández et al., 2017]. To many, this was the realization, through a community of enthusiastic volunteers and institutions, of a global, decentralized, and publicly available Knowledge Graph.

Further reading   To know more about Knowledge Graphs and Linked Data we forward you to the following sources.

- On Knowledge Graphs, the recent survey by Hogan et al. [2021] is a key contribution to condense all ideas, technologies, and methods published under this flag until 2021. Its size (136 pages!) reflects the titanic effort it represents to cover all what *Knowledge Graphs* really encompass. This reference is highly recommended.

- To know more about the history of Knowledge Graphs, see the insightful ISWC 2019 tutorial *Knowledge Graphs: how did we get here?*[3] [Gutierrez and Sequeda, 2020].

---

[2]https://www.w3.org/DesignIssues/LinkedData.html
[3]Juan F. Sequeda and Claudio Gutierrez. *Knowledge Graphs: How did we get here? A Half Day Tutorial on the History of Knowledge Graph's Main Ideas*, ISWC 2019, October 27, 2019. http://knowledgegraph.today.

- Other notable graph databases include Neo4j and the Cyhper query language,[4] Gremlin,[5] and GraphQL (which we introduce later in this chapter in Section 1.4).

1.2   RDF: RESOURCE DESCRIPTION FRAMEWORK

So, as we have just seen, a possible implementation of Knowledge Graphs is through the Web data publishing paradigm of Linked Data, and the third Linked Data principle asks us to provide, upon URI lookups, useful information about a resource in RDF. So: *What is RDF?*

RDF, the Resource Description Framework, is "a language for representing information about resources in the World Wide Web" [Schreiber et al., 2014]. Resources can be anything, really: documents, persons, coffee mugs, buildings, rock bands; any concept, abstract or concrete to which we can attach an identifying URI. Just as URLs uniquely and globally identify HTML Web pages, URIs uniquely and globally identify resources. For example, if we assume that Tim Berners-Lee's URI is https://www.w3.org/People/Berners-Lee/, and that we can abbreviate the W3C domain name (https://www.w3.org/People/) as w3c, the following RDF statements

```
<w3c:Berners-Lee> <rdf:type> <foaf:Person> .
<w3c:Berners-Lee> <foaf:mbox> <mailto:timbl@w3.org> .
```

can be processed by any RDF compliant parser, and tell it that Tim is a person and that his email address is timbl@w3.org. Therefore, RDF statements are made of these short, three-component sentences that we call **triples**. The first element of the triple is the **subject** (i.e., the resource we want to say something about), the second is the **predicate** (i.e., the verb or property on that subject), and the third is the **object** (i.e., the value of that property or the receptor of the statement). **Resources**, in the form of URIs, can appear as subjects, predicates, or objects. **Literals** (e.g., strings, integers, dates, etc.) can appear only in the object position (for example to specify a birth date, an age, or a name). We can also use anonymous URIs in RDF, also known as **blank nodes**, if we don't know—or don't want to create—the URI for a particular resource.

Some of these statements may contain semantically enhanced resources, e.g., terms of the RDFS [Brickley and Guha, 2014] and OWL [McGuinness et al., 2004] vocabularies allow reasoners to derive triples that are only implied by those terms. RDF Knowledge Graphs are practically written down using a number of serializations, like N-Triples, N-Quads, Turtle, or JSON-LD (which embeds RDF into the popular JSON data format).

N-Triples   N-Triples [Beckett, 2014] is an RDF serialization format that emphasizes ease of processing by applications, especially streaming. The basic ideas of N-Triples are: (a) one line, one triple; (b) subjects, predicates, and objects are separated by blank spaces, and triples end with a full stop (.);

---

[4]Neo4j official guide: https://neo4j.com/developer/cypher/guide-cypher-basics/.
[5]Gremlin official guide: https://tinkerpop.apache.org/docs/current/tutorials/getting-started/.

and (c) each line should be fully interpretable in its own (i.e., no prefixes or aliases declared elsewhere). An example is shown in Listing 1.1.

```
<http://dbpedia.org/resource/AC/DC> <http://www.w3.org
    /1999/02/22-rdf-syntax-ns#type> <http://dbpedia.org/ontology/
    Band> .
<http://dbpedia.org/resource/AC/DC> <http://dbpedia.org/ontology/
    genre> <http://dbpedia.org/resource/Hard_rock> .
<http://dbpedia.org/resource/AC/DC> <http://dbpedia.org/ontology/
    genre> <http://dbpedia.org/resource/Blues_rock> .
<http://dbpedia.org/resource/AC/DC> <http://dbpedia.org/ontology/
    activeYearsStartYear> "1973"^^<http://www.w3.org/2001/
    XMLSchema#gYear> .
```

Listing 1.1: Some RDF statements (triples) serialized as N-Triples.

Turtle   Contrarily to N-Triples, the Turtle (Terse RDF Triple Language) serialization [Beckett, 2014] prioritizes human readability in front of ease of automated processing. Turtle introduces several aliasing techniques to make RDF triples shorter and more readable to humans:

- URI namespaces can be aliased through the @prefix keyword.

- If we want to repeat the **subject** of this triple in the next one, we can omit it altogether by finishing the current triple with a semi-colon (;).

- If we want to repeat the **subject and predicate** of this triple in the next one, we can omit both altogether by finishing the current triple with a comma (,).

- Triples end with a full stop (.).

This gives a much more natural reading of RDF, in particular to English speakers; an example is shown in Listing 1.2.

```
@prefix dbr: <http://dbpedia.org/resource/> .
@prefix dbo: <http://dbpedia.org/ontology/Band> .
@prefix xsd: <http://www.w3.org/2001/XMLSchema#> .

dbr:AC/DC a dbo:Band ;
        dbo:genre dbr:Hard_rock , dbr:Blues_rock ;
        dbo:activeYearsStartYear "1973"^^xsd:gYear .
```

Listing 1.2: Some RDF statements (triples) serialized as Turtle.

N-Quads   N-Quads is a similar serialization to N-Triples in the sense that it prioritizes machine read-ability and a line-by-line coherent, independent processing. On top of this, N-Quads adds a fourth "col-umn" to indicate the *named graph* the triple belongs to, after the one indicating the object (remember RDF statements are made of subject, predicate, object triples). This effectively modifies the basic model of RDF, replacing the notion of subject-object-predicate "triples" with subject-object-predicate-graph "quads." The fourth URI, the named graph, allows a higher level of grouping and building sets of triples, allowing triples to be repeated in different graphs if so desired. An example is shown in Listing 1.3.

```
<http://dbpedia.org/resource/AC/DC> <http://www.w3.org
    /1999/02/22-rdf-syntax-ns#type> <http://dbpedia.org/ontology/
    Band> <http://bands.org/awesome-bands> .
<http://dbpedia.org/resource/AC/DC> <http://dbpedia.org/ontology/
    genre> <http://dbpedia.org/resource/Hard_rock> <http://bands.
    org/awesome-bands> .
<http://dbpedia.org/resource/AC/DC> <http://dbpedia.org/ontology/
    genre> <http://dbpedia.org/resource/Blues_rock> <http://bands.
    org/awesome-bands> .
<http://dbpedia.org/resource/AC/DC> <http://dbpedia.org/ontology/
    activeYearsStartYear> "1973"^^<http://www.w3.org/2001/
    XMLSchema#gYear> <http://bands.org/awesome-bands> .
```

Listing 1.3: Some RDF statements with named graphs (quads) serialized as N-Quads.

JSON-LD   Among standard serializations of RDF, JSON-LD is the one developed thinking to web application scenarios. Based on the JSON format, it provides some special attributes for explicit the semantic of the data. In particular, the id and type of a resource can be specified in the @id and @type fields. The other property-values pairs reflect the predicate-object part of the triples, with the predicate to be disambiguated against the schema specified in the context. The latter can be a mapping of each property to a particular URI or a reference to an external schema. Literals can be expressed as plain string or object containing a @value and—optionally—a @type or a @language.

The following example contains some data about AC/DC in JSON-LD.

```
{
  "@context": "http://dbpedia.org/ontology/",
  "@graph": {
    "@id": "http://dbpedia.org/resource/AC/DC",
    "@type": "http://dbpedia.org/ontology/Band",
    "genre": [
      "http://dbpedia.org/resource/Hard_rock",
```

```
        "http://dbpedia.org/resource/Blues_rock"
    ],
    "activeYearsStartYear": {
      "@value": "1973",
      "@type":
        "http://www.w3.org/2001/XMLSchema#gYear"
    }
  }
}
```

Listing 1.4: Some RDF data, serialized as JSON-LD.

Further reading   To know more about Knowledge Graphs and Linked Data we forward you to:

- the *Linked Data: Evolving the Web into a Global Data Space* book [Heath and Bizer, 2011], totally available online in HTML free of charge. To many, this was the canonical technical manual to publish Linked Data in RDF on the Web;

- the RDF 1.1 Primer document[6] [Schreiber et al., 2014] is a nice introduction to the basic concepts and syntax of RDF;

- the official W3C standard specification for RDF Turtle 1.1[7] [Beckett, 2014]; and

- Harald Sack's essential course on YouTube https://www.youtube.com/channel/UCjkkhNSNuXrJpMYZoeSBw6Q/.

1.3   SPARQL: SPARQL PROTOCOL AND RDF QUERY LANGUAGE

SPARQL, a recursive acronym for *SPARQL Protocol and RDF Query Language*, is the standard language for accessing and manipulating RDF data. SPARQL queries are sent over HTTP to a so-called *SPARQL Endpoint*, the HTTP interface of an RDF triplestore.

SPARQL provides several query forms, the most common of which is SELECT, which returns the set of solutions to the conditions expressed in the WHERE clause. These conditions are represented using triple patterns (and their combination): the terms of a triple are **URIs** (often in the prefixed form) and **variables** (introduced by ?) of which we want to obtain the possible values. As an example, the following query can be sent to the DBpedia SPARQL endpoint (https://dbpedia.org/sparql) to produce a list (set of solutions) of all variables that matches the conditions: objects with rdf:type being dbo:Band, where rdf: and dbo: prefixes are declared on the top of the query.

---

[6]RDF 1.1 Primer: https://www.w3.org/TR/rdfa-primer/.
[7]RDF Turtle 1.1 specification: https://www.w3.org/TR/turtle/.

```
PREFIX dbo: <http://dbpedia.org/ontology/>
PREFIX rdf: <http://www.w3.org/1999/02/22-rdf-syntax-ns#>

SELECT ?band WHERE {
  ?band rdf:type dbo:Band .
} LIMIT 100
```

Listing 1.5: Minimal example of a SPARQL SELECT query. PREFIX works analogously to Turtle's @prefix; notice the slight difference in syntax.

The following triple matches these conditions and could be included in the result set.

```
<http://dbpedia.org/resource/AC/DC> rdf:type dbo:Band
```

Listing 1.6: Result of previous SPARQL query.

As with other query languages, SPARQL includes many optional modifiers which makes it so powerful: multiple matching conditions can be combined in a single query by using the UNION modifier; restrictions can be applied to matching condition by using the FILTER modifier; and the LIMIT keyword can be used to obtain an exact maximum number of results.

Apart from SELECT queries, SPARQL includes other kinds of operations such as ASK (which tests the existence of objects matching a specific condition), CONSTRUCT (which allows for building of sub-graphs), DESCRIBE (which returns overview information on a resource), and DELETE (which removes a sub-graph from a triplestore).

A reader with some experience of query languages for databases (e.g., SQL) can understand the SPARQL query examples reported in this book with minimal effort.

Further reading   To further study, we recommend to refer to "Learning SPARQL" [DuCharme, 2013] or to the W3C Specification [W3C SPARQL working group, 2013].

1.4   GRAPHQL: WEB API MADE EASY

A book that aims to speak about Web API cannot avoid a mention about one of the trend technologies in the field: GraphQL.[8]

GraphQL is an approach to develop web APIs, published as open-source software in 2015. Since then, its popularity has largely grown, making it one of the most known JavaScript technology for managing the data layer, and among the most used ones.[9]

---

[8]https://graphql.github.io/
[9]According to the *State of JavaScript 2020* survey. https://2020.stateofjs.com/en-US/technologies/datalayer/.

```
{
    band: {
        name
        genre
        founded_in
    }
}
                          GraphQL Query
```

```
{
    "band": {
        "name": "AC/DC",
        "genre": "Hard Rock",
        "founded_in": 1973
    }
}
                              Results
```

Figure 1.1: Example of GraphQL query and a possible result object.

Its core idea consists of allowing clients to define a template for the required data, in order to return them from the data source, using the desired structure. The API developer is in charge to define the connections between the fields in the data source and the properties available in output for the client. The final user interrogates the API using a query object, whose attributes get a value and are sent back to the client in JSON format. Looking at the example in Figure 1.1, it is possible to notice that only the required properties are retrieved and included in the results, allowing the user to select only the data s/he is interested into.

GraphQL acts as a middleware between the client application and the data source. The latter can be represented by any database, such as SQL, MongoDB, or even a SPARQL endpoint. In this way, GraphQL provides an easy syntax for interrogating any of these databases, invisibly acting behind the scenes and removing any learning curve required for the different query languages.

Further reading   For the scope of this book, only a general knowledge about the GraphQL syntax and behavior is required. For obtaining more information and learning how to use the query language, we recommend the tutorials *An Introduction To GraphQL*[10] and *The Fullstack Tutorial for GraphQL*.[11]

---

[10]Olaf Hartig and Ruben Taelman. An Introduction To GraphQL, Half-day Tutorial at ISWC 2019, October 27, 2019. https://www.ida.liu.se/research/semanticweb/events/GraphQLTutorialAtISWC2019.shtml.

[11]GraphQL Community and Prisma. The Fullstack Tutorial for GraphQL, 2017. https://www.howtographql.com/.

CHAPTER 2

Accessing Knowledge Graphs Programmatically

In Chapter 1 we mentioned some technologies behind Knowledge Graphs (RDF), and the query languages available for accessing their data (SPARQL). These languages use graph-based patterns to specify the criteria under which we want to query the data. Usually, these queries are manually written, tested through trial and error, and incrementally refined and improved until the users gets exactly what is needed.

This kind of workflow—manually crafting and perfecting queries—works just fine for exploratory purposes. When a user is just curious about the contents of a Knowledge Graph, this kind of *user vs. Knowledge Graph* query interaction can be very effective. Queries written this way are usually very specific, and executed only a handful of times.

However, *applications* (Web interfaces, back-end subsystems, Web services, etc.) also need to query Knowledge Graphs for data. Albeit in a slightly different fashion, applications will typically execute these queries thousands of times. In that situation, the *user vs. Knowledge Graph* workflow starts to fall short. Queries do not just need to satisfy the user's curiosity in a singular case; but rather, be prepared to be executed by application logic very often—as often as the application needs. In other words, the query code is not directly written by the curious user anymore; rather, it belongs to the application source code, prepared to be called, repeatedly and automatically, many times.

Moreover, such *application vs. Knowledge Graph* interaction will probably use some sort of query template, instead of requesting something very specific. Developers always try to save lines and write generic source code, following a good software engineering principle. In this case, having too specific queries spread all over the application—e.g., asking about rock and jazz bands that originated either in Los Angeles or in Liverpool—will break this principle. Generic queries and queries using templates or placeholder variables—e.g., asking about music bands of genre x that have y as place of origin—will certainly be more reusable.

When an application needs data from a Knowledge Graph, it typically retrieves it through two separate steps.

1. The application issues a **data request**. This request is done through queries written in a particular query language, for example SPARQL. The difference now is that this query is sent from the application code, which is now responsible for *completing* and *sending* it to a valid endpoint.

2. Manipulate the **data response** received in order to fit the application's purpose. This could consist in changing its format (e.g., from JSON to Python dictionaries), transforming its shape (e.g., what

objects are nested into other objects), or transforming its values (e.g., applying a function that is not supported in the query language to all values).

To complete these two steps, programming languages need support from external libraries that can store, manage, send, process, and transform the results of Knowledge Graph queries. We cover these libraries in this chapter: in Section 2.1 we go over libraries to prepare and send data requests, while in Section 2.2 we focus on libraries to transform data responses.

2.1   QUERYING KNOWLEDGE GRAPHS

In RDF Knowledge Graphs, querying is typically done through SPARQL [W3C SPARQL working group, 2013]. In this section, we show how SPARQL queries can be issued from the application code. We start from basic HTTP requests, and we build up to more complex libraries that encapsulate these requests in growing levels of abstraction.

2.1.1   HTTP REQUESTS

As we have seen in Chapter 1, RDF and SPARQL were built as languages for publishing and querying data on the Web. In particular, SPARQL uses HTTP as a base protocol to send queries to Knowledge Graphs as *HTTP requests*, and to receive the results of such queries as *HTTP responses*. This means that SPARQL can be used to query Knowledge Graphs using any program or library that can deal with HTTP requests.

An HTTP request is made of two elements:

- an **HTTP method** (e.g., GET, POST, PUT, etc.). The method tells the type of action we want to perform on the resource, like retrieving its information (GET) or creating it anew (PUT); and

- an **HTTP resource** (e.g., http://example.org/bands). The resource represents the target of such action.

For example, the hypothetical HTTP request of Listing 2.1 shows an HTTP request that obtains a list of all rock bands known to a certain server.

```
GET http://example.org/bands
```

Listing 2.1: HTTP request retrieving rock bands from a Web API.

For the sake of simplicity we will focus on GET requests as a canonical example for querying. It is important to emphasize that the HTTP resource identifier consists of two parts.

1. The HTTP server. This is the URL prefix that all HTTP resources share in a server; this is, the http://example.org part.

2. The HTTP resource within that server. That is the URL suffix that uniquely identifies the resource with in the server; this is, the `/bands` part.

HTTP uses this syntax to identify different resources within a server—for example, we will likely find information about dogs within that server just replacing `/bands` by `/artists`—but also to introduce an abstraction layer through different servers. If they agree on a common API, it is likely we can use the same trick to get `/bands` and `/artists` from a different HTTP server, e.g., http://rockbands.io.

SPARQL uses this distinction too, albeit with a different nomenclature:

1. a SPARQL HTTP server is called a **SPARQL endpoint**; and

2. a SPARQL HTTP resource is a combination of a **GET parameter** (typically called *query*) and an URL-encoded **SPARQL query**.[1]

For example, let us assume that we want to query the Wikidata [Vrandečić and Krötzsch, 2014] endpoint, `https://query.wikidata.org/sparql`, to get all instances of "rock group" it knows about, using the query shown in Listing 2.2. Property *P31* is *instance of*, and item *Q5741069* are *rock group*.

```
SELECT ?item ?itemLabel
WHERE {
  ?item wdt:P31 wd:Q5741069.
  SERVICE wikibase:label { bd:serviceParam wikibase:language "[
    AUTO_LANGUAGE],en". }
}
```

Listing 2.2: SPARQL query to retrieve all rock groups, and their English labels, from Wikidata.

All we need to do to send this query from an application via HTTP is to compose a URL that concatenates the endpoint name `https://query.wikidata.org/sparql`, the query parameter `?query=`, and the URL-encoded version of the query; and to request that URL with HTTP GET. The result looks like shown in Listing 2.3.

---

[1]For other HTTP-compatible ways of sending queries to SPARQL endpoints, see [W3C SPARQL working group, 2013].

```
GET https://query.wikidata.org/sparql?query=SELECT%20%3Fitem%20%3
    FitemLabel%20%0AWHERE%20%0A%7B%0A%20%20%3Fitem%20wdt%3AP31%20
    wd%3AQ5741069.%0A%20%20SERVICE%20wikibase%3Alabel%20%7B%20bd%3
    AserviceParam%20wikibase%3Alanguage%20%22%5BAUTO_LANGUAGE%5D%2
    Cen%22.%20%7D%0A%7D
```

Listing 2.3: HTTP request retrieving rock groups from the Wikidata SPARQL endpoint service.

This is a well-formed, SPARQL-compliant request that we can issue with any HTTP client or library. For example, curl is a CLI program that can transfer this HTTP requests and show its response, as shown in Listing 2.4.

```
curl -H'Accept: application/json' -X GET "https://query.wikidata.
    org/sparql?query=SELECT%20%3Fitem%20%3FitemLabel%20%0AWHERE
    %20%0A%7B%0A%20%20%3Fitem%20wdt%3AP31%20wd%3AQ5741069.%0A
    %20%20SERVICE%20wikibase%3Alabel%20%7B%20bd%3AserviceParam%20
    wikibase%3Alanguage%20%22%5BAUTO_LANGUAGE%5D%2Cen%22.%20%7D%0A
    %7D"
```

Listing 2.4: Using curl to transfer HTTP data about rock groups from the Wikidata SPARQL endpoint. We set the HTTP header Accept to ask the endpoint to send back the response in JSON format.

curl is convenient for trying HTTP requests out from a terminal interface, but not so much for executing SPARQL queries from the application code. Fortunately, there are plenty of libraries for HTTP requests in a variety of programming languages. There are too many for us to illustrate in this book, so we will use a prototypical example in Python and the requests[2] library. Listing 2.5 shows how this is done, freeing developers from having to manually concatenate URLs of HTTP servers and resources, URL-encode parameters, etc. All we need is two strings to hard-code the SPARQL endpoint address and the body of the SPARQL query, and to let the library know that this query is the value of a parameter named *query* that should be sent as payload. We can also set another dictionary with optional request headers to request the data in, e.g., JSON format, as we did with curl in Listing 2.4. The body of the response from the server is then available to the application to continue its flow.

2.1.2   SPARQL LIBRARIES

In the previous section, we have seen how to send SPARQL queries over HTTP. This can be good enough if our application needs a limited amount of Knowledge Graph data, and we only plan to have a handful of hard-coded strings encoding SPARQL queries in our source code.

[2]https://requests.readthedocs.io/en/master/

```
import requests

endpoint_url = "https://query.wikidata.org/sparql"
query_string = "SELECT ?item ?itemLabel WHERE { ?item wdt:P31 wd:
    Q5741069.  SERVICE wikibase:label { bd:serviceParam wikibase:
    language \"[AUTO_LANGUAGE],en\". }}"

params = {'query' : query_string}
headers = {'accept' : 'application/json'}
r = requests.get(endpoint_url, params=params, headers=headers)

print(r.text)
```

Listing 2.5: Send a SPARQL query to Wikidata via HTTP using the Python library `requests`.

However, applications that need to retrieve huge amounts of data via SPARQL according to a large number of constraints and requirements may be limited by this. As queries grow in size, complexity, and use over our code, it will become increasingly important to generalize and parametrize them—so they are fit for multiple purposes. For example, we may want the same query to have a parameter-set page size through manipulating `OFFSET` and `LIMIT`, or to let us `FILTER` by a user-specified value.

A large number of client-side SPARQL libraries exist for many programming languages, allowing for increasing levels of SPARQL query manipulation, and some degree of generalization and parametrization into what many call, rather than SPARQL queries, *SPARQL templates*. In this section, we review some of these libraries. For a more complete and up-to-date list, we forward the reader to https://github.com/semantalytics/awesome-semantic-web.

SPARQL Wrapper
SPARQL Wrapper[3] is a popular library for sending SPARQL queries and processing their results in Python.

We can better understand the approach of SPARQL Wrapper looking back to the Python examples using `requests` in Section 2.1.1. Listing 2.6 shows how to use SPARQL Wrapper to achieve a similar result. In this case, the constructor `SPARQLWrapper` expects the URL of the SPARQL endpoint to be queried; in the example, we use DBpedia, another large-scale Knowledge Graph of world knowledge extracted from Wikipedia. Next, the `setQuery` method expects a string encoding the SPARQL query to send; in the example, we want to retrieve the human-readable label for the resource representing the city of Barcelona. An interesting feature of SPARQL Wrapper is that it lets us set the return format of the data in the response using the `setReturnFormat` method. JSON will be the preferred option for most

[3]https://rdflib.dev/sparqlwrapper/

developers, but other options like XML are definitely possible.[4] Finally, we execute the query—under the hood, the library will take care of all details around preparing the HTTP request and receiving and converting the response—and we iterate over the result dictionary. An important consideration is that the dictionary keys "results", "bindings", and "value" are static and will not change regardless of the query's contents.[5] However, the key "label" gets its name from the query's variable ?label and we carefully need to adapt it if we change that variable in the query.

RDFLib

RDFLib[6] allows developers to create and manipulate RDF, but also lets them query RDF data using SPARQL, in a slightly different manner. Many times, rather than a SPARQL endpoint, we need to query a file-like source of RDF data, for example a local N-triples file [Beckett, 2014] or a remote HTML page with embedded RDFa [Herman et al., 2015]. In such cases, using RDFLib for querying and processing can be quite useful. Listing 2.7 shows how to do this, assuming there is a public RDF N-triples file at http://example.org/rdf-data.nt with some information about music bands. We start by creating a Graph() object, which can parse() any file-like object containing RDF data; this can be a local or a remote file, even an HTML page with embedded RDFa triples. query() requires the SPARQL query as a string and will take care of locally resolving it against the retrieved data.

```
from SPARQLWrapper import SPARQLWrapper, JSON

sparql = SPARQLWrapper("http://dbpedia.org/sparql")
sparql.setQuery("""
    PREFIX rdfs: <http://www.w3.org/2000/01/rdf-schema#>
    SELECT ?label
    WHERE {
     <http://dbpedia.org/resource/Barcelona> rdfs:label ?label
    }""")
sparql.setReturnFormat(JSON)
results = sparql.query().convert()

for result in results["results"]["bindings"]:
    print(result["label"]["value"])
```

Listing 2.6: Sending a SPARQL query to an endpoint with SPARQL Wrapper.

---

[4]Note here that: (a) in the HTTP example we achieved a similar result by directly manipulating the contents of the Accept HTTP header; and (b) not all SPARQL endpoints will support all content negotiation formats.

[5]We will see this in deep in Chapter 5.

[6]https://rdflib.readthedocs.io/en/stable/

```
import rdflib

g = rdflib.Graph()
g.parse("http://example.org/rdf-data.nt")

qres = g.query(
    """
    PREFIX dbo: <http://dbpedia.org/ontology/>
    PREFIX rdf: <http://www.w3.org/1999/02/22-rdf-syntax-ns#>
    PREFIX rdfs: <http://www.w3.org/2000/01/rdf-schema#>

    SELECT ?bandname
    WHERE {
        ?a rdf:type dbo:Band ;
           rdfs:label ?bandname .
    }""")

for row in qres:
    print(row)
```

Listing 2.7: Retrieving file-like RDF data (local or remote) and querying it with SPARQL and RDFLib.

RDFLib offers other interesting ways of querying RDF data using Basic Graph Pattern (BGP) matching, instead of SPARQL syntax. The example shown in Listing 2.8 is analogous to that shown in Listing 2.7, but uses the `triples()` iterator[7] to match resources of type dbo:Band and then iterates over the labels for such resources, producing the same result.

---

[7]Note that: (a) the `triples()` iterator requires a Python tuple as a parameter of the form (s, p, o), matching the shape of a triple pattern; and (b) the None Python keyword is used to specify the unknown resource(s) of the query—which typically are SPARQL variables.

```
import rdflib
from rdflib import URIRef
from rdflib.namespace import RDF, RDFS

g = rdflib.Graph()
g.parse("http://example.org/rdf-data.nt")

for s,p,o in g.triples((None, RDF.type,
                URIRef("http://dbpedia.org/ontology/Band"):
    for u,v,s in g.triples((s, RDFS.label, None)):
        print(s)
```

Listing 2.8: Retrieving file-like RDF data (local or remote) and querying it using RDFLib iterators.

Jena

Apache Jena[8] is a Java framework which provides similar functionality to that provided by *RDFLib* and *SPARQL Wrapper* libraries in Python, via its ARQ query engine.

Jena is a full framework, with different APIs including a SPARQL server and semantic reasoning engine, making it a very powerful SPARQL library.

2.2   MANIPULATING SPARQL'S OUTPUT

After having executed a query SPARQL endpoint, the next obvious step is to use the obtained result. Previously mentioned libraries like RDFLib and Jena are equipped with data manipulation capabilities. In this section, we move the focus to web application development and introduce some standards and tools for manipulating SPARQL results in JavaScript. Those tools have been chosen in order to introduce different manipulation paradigms, from replicating the graph in the JavaScript environment to directly choose the desired output template.

RDFJS and rdflib.js

RDFJS[9] is a set of specifications published by the W3C's RDF JavaScript Libraries Community Group. The core of the proposal is the *RDF/JS: Data model specification*, finalized in 2020. It is a low-level specification, including common abstract interfaces to serve as a guide for implementation.

The model aims to represent data keeping the graph structure, which is then directly manipulated by the developer. The atomic information is the *Term*, an abstract element representing any node or edge in the graph. A *Term* is instantiated in one of the interface's extensions: *NamedNode, BlankNode,*

---

[8]https://jena.apache.org/index.html
[9]https://rdf.js.org/

```
import org.apache.jena.query.*;

public class JenaTest {
    public static void main(String []args) {
        String endpoint = "http://dbpedia.org/sparql";
        String queryString =
    "PREFIX rdfs: <http://www.w3.org/2000/01/rdf-schema#>\n" +
    "SELECT ?label \n" +
    "WHERE {  \n" +
    "<http://dbpedia.org/resource/Barcelona> rdfs:label ?label"
    + "\n }";

        Query query = QueryFactory.create(queryString);
        QueryExecution qexec = QueryExecutionFactory.
            sparqlService(endpoint, query);
        try {
            ResultSet results = qexec.execSelect();
            ResultSetFormatter.out( results );
        }
        finally {
            qexec.close();
        }
    }
}
```

Listing 2.9: Sending a SPARQL query to an endpoint with Jena.

Literal, *Variable* (intended to be used in queries), and *DefaultGraph*. The RDF triple is encapsulated in a *Quad*, which requires a subject term, a predicate term, and an object term, as well as the graph the triple belongs to. The *DataFactory* object contains methods to create terms and quads.

Different libraries implement the RDFJS data model, among which **rdflib.js** is quite known in the community. The data is extracted from a data store, initialized with $rdf.graph(). The content of the store can be created directly in the code (as in Listing 2.10), fetched from the Web, or read from a local file. The data is inserted or selected using the triple format (subject, predicate, object). Literals can be expressed as strings, while named nodes are created using the $rdf.sym() function.

In queries, the JavaScript undefined keyword can be used as a wildcard for marking the variable, whose values we want to retrieve. Rdflib.js provides two convenient methods for obtaining all matching results (each) or just the first one (any).

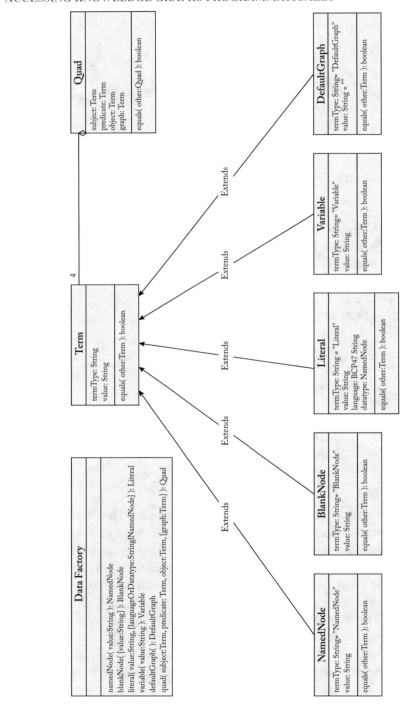

Figure 2.1: Interface schema of RDFJS.

In addition to the described features, rdflib.js includes a data fetcher, a parser, data serializers (for RDF XML, Turtle, JSON-LD, etc.) and the `Namespace` class for easily declaring and using prefixes.

```javascript
// Define the DBO namespace
var DBO = Namespace("http://dbpedia.org/ontology/");
var RDFS = Namespace("http://www.w3.org/2000/01/rdf-schema#");

// The store is the object that contains all triples
var store = $rdf.graph();


var band = $rdf.sym('http://dbpedia.org/resource/AC/DC');

// Insert triples in the store
store.add(band, RDFS('label'), 'AC/DC');
store.add(band, DBO('genre'),
        $rdf.sym('http://dbpedia.org/resource/Hard_rock'));
store.add(band, DBO('genre'),
        $rdf.sym("http://dbpedia.org/resource/Rock_and_roll"));

// Retrieve all (each) or one (any) results, using wildcards
var genres = store.each(band, DBO('genre'), undefined)
for (var genre of genres)
    console.log(genre.uri);
```

Listing 2.10: Creating and manipulating RDF data in rdflib.js.

LDFlex

LDFlex is a library for RDF data access and manipulation in JavaScript, built following the RDFJS specification. The goal of LDFlex[10] is to provide the user a way of "querying Linked Data on the Web as if you were browsing a local JavaScript graph" [Verborgh and Taelman, 2020]. This work is fully integrated into the Comunica framework [Taelman et al., 2018a] and the Solid ecosystem [Verborgh, 2020].

In the LDFlex *local graph paradigm*, the user can navigate the graph by accessing the attributed of a JavaScript object. For example, `band.genre.label` would retrieve the labels of the genres played by band. The semantics is disambiguated through a JSON-LD context, which maps each attribute to an RDF predicate (see Chapter 1).

---

[10]https://ldflex.github.io/LDflex/

When an attribute is accessed, LDFlex intercepts the operation through *JavaScript Proxies,*[11] which execute a function (called *handler*) which computes the actual attribute value. In particular, the function constructs a SPARQL query using the information of the context, executes it and returns the solution. In other words, the Proxies are used to "disguise" the queries as attributes. JavaScript native `async/await` syntax makes sure that the results are obtained before moving to the next instruction. In this way, the query mechanic ends up being totally transparent to the developer.

> **Promises and async/await in JavaScript.** The communication between JavaScript applications and SPARQL endpoints generally runs over HTTP requests. These requests are executed asynchronously, while the JavaScript engine can be dedicated to other jobs. Once the HTTP response has been received, a so-called *callback function* is executed, in order to process the obtained results. This pipeline can also be implemented using a *Promise*, an object which assumes a *pending* state waiting for the asynchronous function to return, with the "promise" (in fact) of a result at some point in future. The proxy's handler of LDFlex returns a Promise, which is resolved when the query is executed and results are obtained.
>
> The `async` keyword is used for declaring a function that returns a Promise. In addition to this, it enables the use of the `await` keyword, which can only be used inside `async` functions. When a Javascript expression is prepended with `await`—like in `var res = await getResults()`—, the code execution is suspended until the Promise is resolved. When available, the final value is automatically assigned to the involved variable—`res` in our example. In this way, it is possible to write the code as a sequence of "synchronous" instructions, even if the values are obtained asynchronously.

In addition to the described behavior, LDFlex provides ways for sorting the results, updating the data, etc. The query engine is not part of the library, for which the use of Comunica is recommended. Listing 2.11 shows an example of usage of the module.

---

[11]ECMAScript 2017 Language Specification (ECMA-262, 8th edition, June 2017) https://262.ecma-international.org/8.0/.

```
const { PathFactory } = require('ldflex');
const { default: ComunicaEngine } = require('@ldflex/comunica');
const { namedNode } = require('@rdfjs/data-model');

// The context maps properties and URIs
const context = {
  "@context": {
    "@vocab": "http://dbpedia.org/ontology/",
    "label": "http://www.w3.org/2000/01/rdf-schema#label",
  }
};

// The query engine interact with the SPARQL endpoint
const endpoint = 'http://dbpedia.org/sparql';
const queryEngine = new ComunicaEngine(endpoint);

// The PathFactory is the access point to the data
const path = new PathFactory({ context, queryEngine });

// define the band node as subject for queries
const band = path.create({
  subject: namedNode('http://dbpedia.org/resource/AC/DC') });
getGenres(band);

async function getGenres(band) {
  // Under the hood, SPARQL queries are executed
  console.log(`This band is ${await band.label}`);

  console.log(`${await band.label} usually plays:`);
  for await (const genre of band.genre.label)
    console.log(`- ${genre}`);
}
```

Listing 2.11: Manipulating RDF data in LDFlex.

```
{                                   GraphQL Query
  label @single
  album {
    label
  }
  genre(label_en: "Hard rock") @single
}
```

```
{                                                        JSON-LD context
  "@context": {
    "label": "http://www.w3.org/2000/01/rdf-schema#label",
    "label_en": { "@id": "http://www.w3.org/2000/01/rdf-schema#label", "@language": "en" },
    "album": { "@reverse": "http://dbpedia.org/ontology/album" },
    "genre": "http://dbpedia.org/ontology/genre"
  }
}
```

Figure 2.2: A query in GraphQL-LD, with its related context.

GraphQL-Based Strategies

Several SPARQL interfaces for GraphQL have been proposed so far, following different strategies [Taelman et al., 2019]. Some of these solutions rely on automatic mappings of variables to property names (Stardog[12]), while others rely on a context (GraphQL-LD[13]) or a schema (HyperGraphQL[14]).

In **GraphQL-LD** [Taelman et al., 2018b], the disambiguation of properties is controlled by a JSON-LD context, which contains the mapping of each property to a URI—similarly to what we have seen for LDFlex. A special syntax can be used for filtering by language (combination of @id and @language), changing the predicate direction (@reverse), obtaining a single result rather that a list (@single), as it is possible to appreciate in Figure 2.2. The library combines the information in the query and in the context for computing the equivalent SPARQL query, sent to the SPARQL endpoint. The results are then applied to the query object structure and returned.

HyperGraphQL requires a schema definition and a configuration file. The latter contains a list of SPARQL endpoints—called *services*—that the API needs to query, together with some preference for setting up the API server. The schema definition includes a context for mapping properties to URIs. In addition, every type and property can be assigned to a specific server, allowing federated queries. The results are wrapped in a more complex object, including metadata such as the used context. Figure 2.3 shows an example of configuration, schema, and query in HyperGraphQL.

---

[12]https://www.stardog.com/
[13]https://github.com/rubensworks/graphql-to-sparql.js
[14]https://www.hypergraphql.org

```
{                                        Configuration
    "name": "my-api",
    "schema": "schema.graphql",
    "server": {
        "port": 8080,
        "graphql": "/graphql",
        "graphiql": "/graphiql"
    },
    "services": [{
        "id": "dbpedia-sparql",
        "type": "SPARQLEndpointService",
        "url": "http://dbpedia.org/sparql/",
        "graph": "http://dbpedia.org",
        "user": "",  "password": ""
    }]
}
```

```
                                         GraphQL Query
{
  Band_GET(limit: 1) {
    _id
    _type
    label
    genre {
      _id
      label(lang: "en")
    }
  }
}
```

```
type __Context {
    Band:  _@href(iri: "http://dbpedia.org/ontology/Band")
    Genre: _@href(iri: "http://dbpedia.org/ontology/Genre")
    label: _@href(iri: "http://www.w3.org/2000/01/rdf-schema#label")
    genre: _@href(iri: "http://dbpedia.org/ontology/genre")
}
type Band @service(id:"dbpedia-sparql") {
    label: [String] @service(id:"dbpedia-sparql")
    genre: Genre @service(id:"dbpedia-sparql")
}
type Genre @service(id:"dbpedia-sparql") {
    label: [String] @service(id:"dbpedia-sparql")
                                         Schema definition
}
```

Figure 2.3: Configuration, schema, and query in HyperGraphQL

CHAPTER 3

Web Data APIs Over SPARQL

In Chapter 2 we saw how to query Knowledge Graphs with SPARQL from within application code, either directly using HTTP, or by resorting to one of the various SPARQL libraries available for programming languages. This has provided us with some additional tools, on top of just manually writing and executing queries, toward their generalization and parametrization: in large applications we need query templates to avoid query re-writing.

This is a powerful paradigm: combining the expressivity of SPARQL—which allows access to a large set of openly available Knowledge Graphs, as seen in Chapter 1—with a rich ecosystem of protocols and libraries to execute, parametrize, and abstract queries in application code, developers can retrieve semantically rich data for their applications with literally a handful of lines of code.

So, what is the problem with this? Why aren't the vast majority of Web developers using SPARQL from within application code? One part of the answer is: there is no problem, and they *should* be using more SPARQL! However, this answer neglects important parts of the bigger picture. The truth is that not every developer will be keen on learning SPARQL to gain the ability to query Knowledge Graphs. This might be due to a number of social and economic reasons, including budget and time constraints, library coupling, or even principle. The fact is that the requirement of having to learn SPARQL can be a barrier for developers that want to query Knowledge Graphs. Research has tried to address this in various ways, e.g., by building graphical interfaces on top of SPARQL. We will be addressing—or rather, mitigating—this barrier later in the book in Chapter 4, with query management and sharing.

The other reason for developers to stay away from querying Knowledge Graphs with SPARQL is the plausible alternative of REST APIs. While the Semantic Web was in its early days, a different approach for querying Web data took shape and quickly became the overwhelmingly common way to consume remote data on the Web: representational state transfer, or REST, APIs[1] [Fielding and Taylor, 2000]. REST APIs allow one to "manipulate textual representations of Web resources by using a uniform and predefined set of stateless operations," and therefore provide a simple interface to obtain and manipulate remote Web resources. Much simpler, in fact, than SPARQL. However, this simplicity comes at a price: REST APIs give away almost any expressive power in their queries, telling developers precisely what data can be queried and how, and therefore downgrading how much choice developers have at the client side [Haupt et al., 2015]. Perhaps out of pure pragmatism this seemed not to be an issue for most developers that embraced the RESTful API paradigm. In production development en-

---

[1] Despite REST has a precise definition and not every Web API is a REST API, we will be using both terms *REST API* and *Web API* in this book, highlighting the differences in every instance.

vironments, and outside the context of the Semantic Web and Knowledge Graphs, REST APIs are the industry standard.

This apparent dichotomy between SPARQL and RESTful APIs lies at the core of this book, and is specifically addressed in Chapters 4 and 5. Are these two models of Web querying irreconcilable? Is it possible to offer developers ways to benefit from the two? Previous research benefits from the integration space that Knowledge Graphs offer.

An exemplary case is the OpenPHACTS platform [Williams et al., 2012], which builds an API layer on top of its SPARQL endpoint, between SPARQL and application requests (see Figure 3.1). This kind of stacked, separation-of-concerns (SoC) based architecture is the foundation of the methods, techniques, and tools we will be diving into in Chapters 4 and 5. But before we do that, we need to gain a better understanding of the building blocks of such an architecture and their interactions: Web Data API specifications; the build-up of such specifications for SPARQL-accessible Knowledge Graphs; and the pros and cons of taking this approach.

3.1   REST APIS

Contrarily to SPARQL endpoints, which allow clients to send any query, REST APIs manage the interaction with data consumers in two steps.

1. They *define* and expose what resources and methods (see Section 2.1.1) are allowed (also known as the API documentation or "API docs").

2. They *receive* the HTTP requests against those allowed resources and methods, process them, and return a result to the client.

An example of an API doc about rock bands is shown in Figure 3.2. The first route is GET /bands/, and its descriptions suggest that this will return a list of all available rock bands behind the API. Conversely, the next one, POST /bands/, will create a new band in the backend (possibly asking details about such a band as parameters, as we'll see later; and surely asking clients to be authenticated). The documentation goes on in the various ways in which clients may ask details about a specific rock band (GET /bands/{band_id/}/), update its details (with HTTP PUT), delete it, etc.

Originally, API docs were manually written by developers in HTML as technical documentation, so they could communicate to other developers what routes were available at their servers, what parameters should be used in every route, etc. With time, this became an increasingly tiresome task that API publishers wanted to automate. This is how API documentations quickly became **API specifications** in need of standardization.

3.1.1   THE OPENAPI SPECIFICATION

The OpenAPI specification,[2] previously known as the Swagger specification,[3] is the industry standard for creating and publishing API definitions in a structured way. Moreover, the fact that the specification

---

[2]https://www.openapis.org
[3]https://swagger.io

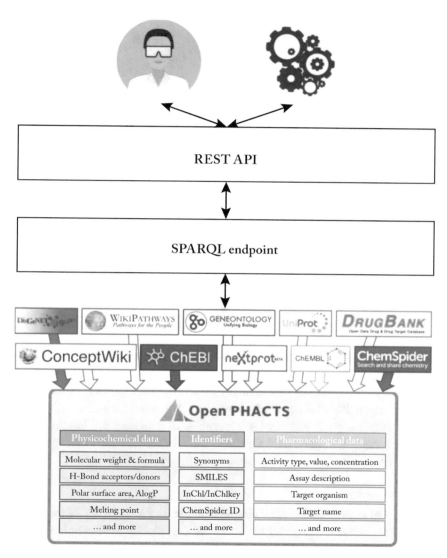

Figure 3.1: Overall concepts behind the OpenPHACTS architecture for enabling Knowledge Graph access through REST APIs. The main idea is to build a Knowledge Graph to integrate information from various sources; use SPARQL on top to leverage that integrated data space; and build a REST API layer on top of SPARQL to enable easy consumption by users and applications.

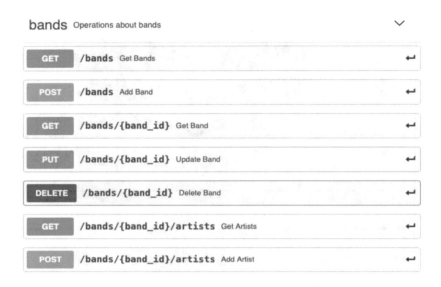

Figure 3.2: An example of an API doc, listing the routes (combinations of resources and methods) that are available for clients to call about rock bands.

can be implemented in YAML or JSON makes it especially suitable for developers to "embed" some of its parts directly into application code.[4]

    This book is not a REST API manual; by the time it's published, newer versions (or other standards) probably will make our content outdated. We refer the reader to the online resources at https://www.openapis.org for full details. Nevertheless, provided the importance this specification presently has for the task at hand (and for the techniques we will see in Chapter 4), we will describe here its basic components.

Metadata and Server Routes

The first sections of any OpenAPI specification, either in its YAML or JSON form, describe the general metadata about the API and the server routes it makes available. An example is shown in Listing 3.1. Specifically, *metadata* fields indicate the OpenAPI specification version the API adheres to, which may be useful to inform consumers of its features; and the title, description, and version of the API, which will mainly inform humans of what the API does and its development status. *Server routes* are used to indicate the URLs that must be used as a base namespace when using the API, and to which the *path* (or method) names must be appended to. These URLs are usually unique, as one API is typically based

---

[4]See https://swagger.io/tools/open-source/open-source-integrations/ for a list of open source libraries.

```
openapi: 3.0.0
info:
  title: Music Bands API
  description: Provides information about music bands. This
      description supports [CommonMark](http://commonmark.org/) or
      HTML syntax.
  version: 1.2.1
servers:
  - url: http://api.rockbands.io/v1
    description: Main (production) server  # This description is
        optional
  - url: http://staging-api.rockbands.io
    description: Internal staging server for testing # This
        description is optional
```

Listing 3.1: Example of the metadata and server routes sections of an OpenAPI specification.

in one server; but having more might be useful for development purposes (for example, for hosting different production and a testing versions of the API).

Paths, Parameters, and Responses

Following metadata and server routes, the most important part of an OpenAPI specification describes the *paths* it makes available, together with the parameters expected in those paths (if any), and the responses that clients can expect upon success when calling those paths (i.e., when they send an HTTP request to its resources via a supported method). Listing 3.2 shows an example for an API that exposes one single path, /bands/{id}, accessible by the GET HTTP method and that returns information about a music band specified by the client. After indicating the path's name, we can specify the parameters it supports, two in this case: the specific band to retrieve by its identifier, which we know is an integer and must (not optionally, as it's "required") be supplied in the "path" by replacing the {id} placeholder; and an optional includeLocation which is a true/false value supplied as a query parameter—i.e., appended at the end of the URL. All in all, a valid call to this path might look as follows.

```
GET http://api.rockbands.io/v1/bands/32?includeLocation=true
```

```
paths:
  /bands/{band_id}:
    description: Returns a band by its id, and optionally its
        location details
    parameters:
    - name: band_id
      in: path
      required: true
      description: the band identifier
      schema:
        type: integer
    - name: includeLocation
      in: query
      description: whether to return the band's location
      required: false
      schema:
        type: boolean
    get:
      responses:
        '200':
          description: the band being returned
          content:
            application/json:
              schema:
                type: object
                properties:
                  id: # the unique band id
                    type: integer
                  name: # the band's name
                    type: string
                    format: binary
                  location: # the band's location
                    type: string
                    format: binary
```

Listing 3.2: Example of the paths section of an OpenAPI specification.

According to the specification in Listing 3.2, when such a call is successful it will return a 200 response[5] with a well-defined result in its body in JSON format. As defined in the schema section, this result will be one single object with three properties: the band ID (as an integer), the band's name (as a binary string), and the band's location (if we requested it via the query parameter includeLocation). For example (ignoring the HTTP headers):

```
{"id" : 32, "name" : "Led Zeppelin", "location" : "London"}
```

3.1.2   WRITING WEB APIS

Having standards like the OpenAPI specification allows us to quickly build API specifications and documentation. This provides three powerful advantages over writing API documentation manually: it lets us build API documentation automatically; it enormously facilitates interoperability between different APIs; and it enables both machines (through JSON and YAML) and humans (through their HTML derivatives) to consume these API specifications.

However, the one thing these specifications cannot do is the actual implementation of the API: that is, the functions and code that will be executed at the server side whenever HTTP calls are sent to any of the *paths*. After all, APIs are just that: Application Programming Interfaces. As it happens with library APIs, they only expose **what** can be called, how, and what to expect as a result; but it is a good programming principle to hide the implementation details, and leave that concern to the library itself.

So, what does the actual implementation of these paths look like? As the reader may expect, there are hundreds of choices in paradigms, languages, and libraries that could be used for this; for the sake of simplicity, in Listing 3.3 we show an example using Python and Flask, a Web microframework. As the reader will notice, many details of the OpenAPI specification (such as the path description, name, parameters, and response schema) overlap with this implementation. Other libraries can work in conjunction with Flask and elegantly deal with this mapping.

When a client issues an HTTP get to the /bands/{id} path, the Python function band is executed on the server. It gets its parameters by parsing the called URL, either from the path itself (id, which Flask requires to map as a function parameter and hence becomes immediately available in that context) or from the query parameters (includeLocation, which Flask gets from the request.args object). Generally, the next thing to do is to use those parameters to retrieve the solicited data from somewhere else, typically a database engine. In the example, we assume a db object with a prepared connection able to answer SELECT queries, and we use that interface to retrieve the band's details. Importantly, as a next step we would need to post-process the results form the database: this might include data aggregations, transformations, and cleaning; in general, any processing needed to adapt the raw data from the database into values that fit to our declared schema. Then, we fit those post-processed results into such a schema: in this case, by creating a Python dictionary with the fields required by the API schema—the

---

[5]200 is the HTTP code to indicate a successful request.

```
@app.route('/bands/{band_id}', method = ['GET'])
def band(band_id):
    """Returns a band by its id, and optionally its location
        details"""
    includeLocation = request.args['includeLocation'] # Capture
        the optional query parameter
    result = db.select('bands', band_id, includeLocation)
    ... # Some result post-processing as needed
    response = {'id': result.id, 'name': result.name , 'location'
        : result.location }

    return jsonify(response)
```

Listing 3.3: Example of the implementation of an API path in Python, as defined in an excerpt of an OpenAPI specification.

band ID, its name, and its location. Finally, we return an HTTP 200 response with a conversion of that dictionary into a JSON object, which is what the API specification promises.

With an implementation such as this one for each of the *paths* defined in an OpenAPI specification, we can see now how REST APIs, in particular by providing structured, standard specifications, and their accompanying implementations, can function as a communication interface between data consumers (clients, applications) and data providers. The simple combination of HTTP methods (GET, POST, etc.) and resources (/bands/ with its parameters) is a simple yet powerful paradigm to access data, independent of which database engine is used to store this data. How does this fit, then, the picture of querying Knowledge Graphs with SPARQL? In the next sections, we will see how REST APIs may work when data—rather than locally stored in a database—is remotely published in a Knowledge Graph.

3.2   WRITING KNOWLEDGE GRAPH APIS

Using all we have seen about building REST APIs, what would it take to build a REST API that, instead of interfacing with a local database engine, retrieved data from a SPARQL endpoint?

Consider the example we used in the previous section to build an API for our bands database (Listing 3.3). As we have seen, REST APIs work independently of the underlying database technology: this is one of their greatest advantages. So, implementing an API path that retrieves a specified band by ID using SPARQL is just a specific case of the example in Listing 3.3. For the sake of argument, let us assume that we want to do this using Wikidata's SPARQL endpoint—which surely will know about a band named "Led Zeppelin."

An example implementation is shown in Listing 3.4. Actually, this implementation does not differ much from what we saw in the example of Listing 2.5 on sending HTTP requests to SPARQL endpoints. There are, however, some small but important differences. One of them is the need to include specific endpoint details, such as the endpoint URL and the format we want the data in (JSON). But perhaps the most important difference comes from the need for tweaking the SPARQL query that retrieves all bands in Wikidata, and adapting it so it can serve the purpose of asking about *any* band. The query that retrieves all bands in Wikidata is as follows (wd:Q5741069 is the item "rock groups," wdt:P31 is the "instance of" property, and wdt:P740 is the "location of formation" property):

```
SELECT ?item ?itemLabel ?locationLabel
WHERE {
    ?item wdt:P31 wd:Q5741069 .
    ?item wdt:P740 ?location .
    SERVICE wikibase:label {
      bd:serviceParam wikibase:language "[AUTO_LANGUAGE],en" }
}
```

However, we are only interested in a specific band identified by its ID (Led Zeppelin's ID in Wikidata is wdt:Q2331). We could replace all instances of the variable ?item with that ID, but that would include the projection variable right after SELECT, which would be a syntax error. A much more elegant solution is to introduce the VALUES clause, which will defer the job to SPARQL by requesting to include results that bind ?item to the specific values in the clause. The problem is, of course, that we do not know beforehand what these values will be. To solve this, one option we have is to introduce a placeholder ___id___ that will be replaced with the value of the URL parameter band_id. With this placeholder in the query (sometimes hence also called *query template* or *parametrized query*), our API implementation will systematically rewrite it to retrieve the details of the band whose ID has been supplied only, therefore fulfilling the API specification for this particular path.

As the reader can notice, parametrizing queries in this way can be a general and effective method for mapping the requirements of Open/REST API specifications and the particularities of SPARQL queries. SPARQL queries can still grow in complexity, requiring the addition of more API parameter placeholders; and some concrete features of the OpenAPI spec may need to be managed properly, like authentication or write permissions.

But under reasonable assumptions, we could imagine that the average use case for building APIs for Knowledge Graphs essentially consists in repeating this pattern over and over: map the API specification into the function/route headers; map the API parameters into SPARQL VALUES placeholders; send the rewritten query to the specified endpoint and collect the results; and map the results into the desired schema and build the HTTP response. If we further assume that the entire API operate over one single SPARQL endpoint, which is often the case, we may need to ask for the endpoint URL just

```python
@app.route('/bands/{band_id}', method = ['GET'])
def band(band_id):
    """Returns a band by its id, and optionally its location
        details"""

    # Capture the optional query parameter
    includeLocation = request.args['includeLocation']

    endpoint_url = "https://query.wikidata.org/sparql"
    query_string = """
SELECT ?item ?itemLabel ?locationLabel
    WHERE {
        ?item wdt:P31 wd:Q5741069 .
        ?item wdt:P740 ?location .
        VALUES ?item (___id___)
        SERVICE wikibase:label { bd:serviceParam
            wikibase:language "[AUTO_LANGUAGE],en" }
    }"""
    query_string.replace("___id___", id)

    # Prepare HTTP request
    payload = {'query' : query_string}
    headers = {'accept' : 'application/json'}
    r = requests.get(endpoint_url, params=payload, headers=
        headers)

    data = r.json()
    response = {'id': data['item'], 'name': data['itemLabel']}
    if includeLocation:
        response['location'] = data['locationLabel']

    return jsonify(response)
```

Listing 3.4: Example of the implementation of an API path in Python, querying the Wikidata SPARQL endpoint instead of a local database.

once. In other words, we have reduced the complexity of building Knowledge Graph APIs to properly managing, and documenting, a handful of SPARQL queries.

3.3   LIMITATIONS OF KNOWLEDGE GRAPH APIS

As we have seen, combining REST APIs, OpenAPI specifications, and HTTP requests can be a powerful tool to quickly build and deploy SPARQL-based Knowledge Graph APIs. We could leave it at this point, and recommend all developers interested in exposing Knowledge Graph APIs to adapt the example shown in Listing 3.4 to any operation or API path that they want to expose to their clients.

However, such a recommendation would have three very important limitations: repetitive work, query management, and controlling results. The rest of this book explains methods and tools to overcome them.

3.3.1   REPETITIVE WORK

The first limitation of building Knowledge Graph APIs as in Listing 3.4 is that this process does not scale. As we can observe in many APIs, lots and lots of paths are simple, retrieval operations of the type "get all instances of type X" or "get this specific instance with this identifier." Sure, some implementations require some post-hoc data manipulation for transformations that can be cumbersome to implement only in SPARQL—e.g., use the retrieved data to calculate a standard deviation, a correlation value, etc. But for most cases, the SPARQL query *is exactly* the functionality to be implemented. For such cases, writing large Knowledge Graph APIs that merely take SPARQL queries, send them to the endpoint, and return the results may be **too big (and boring) a task to a developer**. If the queries do fully implement all needed functionality, organizing and documenting them properly should suffice for an **automatic generation of their equivalent API specifications and implementations**. We deal with this limitation in Chapter 4.

3.3.2   QUERY MANAGEMENT

Now that we are certain that building a Knowledge Graph API boils down to writing and managing SPARQL queries, an interesting question is: what exactly does query management consist of?

For the developer that manually writes Knowledge Graph APIs, that management probably consists of testing those SPARQL queries on the endpoint until they work—saving them in some text file in their laptop, and copy-pasting them into the API code, mapping parameters as needed. But surely these practices can be further improved: documenting the queries, keeping them under version control, storing them in a source code repository, transparently publishing them on the Web (through e.g., global and unique identifiers), and separately specifying how their variables map into API parameters are all **activities that surely can help in managing these queries better**. Perhaps most importantly, these activities for a neat query management can surely help in improving the separation of concerns of various code layers (e.g., query management, query rewriting, query fetching for APIs, etc.). We deal with query management also in Chapter 4.

3.3.3   CONTROLLING RESULTS

The third limitation of Knowledge Graph APIs built as in Listing 3.4 is that controlling the results of an API path, and in particular the JSON schema they adhere to, is not that simple. For starters, SPARQL is designed to really return schema-less *tables*: result sets are built with the bindings of projection variables in a row-by-row basis. To overcome this limitation, one could imagine creative ways of using the schema section of the OpenAPI specification to automatically build the response dictionary/object so that its shape matches that of the specification. However, this might not be trivial for all schemas, in particular for very complex ones.

Additionally, the schema indicated in the OpenAPI specification might not be good enough for many developers. Sure they need to adhere to that schema in order to correctly parse the results of their requests; but many may be interested in **requesting the data declaratively with the shape they want their JSON responses in**. We present techniques to do this in Chapter 5.

CHAPTER 4

grlc: API Automation by Query Sharing

In Section 3.3, we discussed some of the limitations typically encountered when building Knowledge Graph APIs. In summary, we discussed the following issues:

- repetitive and unsystematic use of queries;

- lack of separation of concerns (query management);

- lack of transparency (query management); and

- difficulty of versioning (query management).

In this chapter, we will focus on the motivation behind *grlc*: a tool for building Linked Data (Knowledge Graph) APIs, with the aim of addressing these issues. We discuss the niche it covers in the Knowledge Graph landscape, provide some examples of its main features, and provide links for further reading.

4.1   OVERVIEW

grlc is an open-source software package which automatically builds Knowledge Graph APIs from a collection of SPARQL queries. It incorporates many features which allow for APIs flexibility (see Section 4.4). This allows *grlc* to tackle the limitations discussed in Section 3.3: a systematic approach to API development avoids repetitive work; queries are stored separately from application source code; queries can be made publicly available on the Web allowing for API transparency; and queries can be stored in GitHub, allowing version controlled APIs.

So, what is the basic idea of *grlc*? Its main tenet is that bringing up Web APIs on top of SPARQL endpoints (as we have seen in Chapter 3) should not be any harder than simply publishing the SPARQL queries implementing the operations of those Web APIs. Very often, such operations do not require anything more or anything less than mapping their API parameters to a SPARQL query, executing that query against the endpoint, and simply returning the results to the user of the API. True, there will be cases that will not adjust to this schema: some complex API operations might require more than one SPARQL query (for example, if the operation needs to grab data from various data sources using different query languages) or may need some pre-processing (for example, to the input parameters or to the queried databases) or post-processing (for example, transforming the data with algorithms that are not supported in SPARQL; or converting the results to another data model). But, in our experience, these cases are rare and, for most users, a one-query SPARQL implementation of the operation is more than enough.

grlc can automatically build Web APIs on top of SPARQL endpoints by leveraging this one-query, one-operation philosophy, and three other important principles.

Avoiding repetitive labor   As we have seen in Chapter 2, writing Web APIs involves a lot of code repetition around language-dependent facilities such as function headers, decorators, parameters, etc., around the API. In most cases, developers are not really interested in these mechanical, language-based translations: they just want to turn their SPARQL queries into a functional Web API.

Leveraging query management and documentation   It turns out that, in many cases, developers are already saving their queries into proper management systems, and not just hard-coding them as we saw in Chapter 2. With just a little bit of additional care in adding the right metadata on top of those queries, they can go from simple text files encoding one query, to central resources in specifying full-fledged, actionable API operations. Most of this chapter assumes that GitHub[1] is such a system; but any other proxy with similar features will do also.

Reusing publicly accessible queries   The key of *grlc* de-coupling with queries is that it does not need to physically store nor confine them to its system. All it needs is that SPARQL queries are publicly available on the Web and de-referenceable via HTTP.[2] This brings up a unique, interesting feature of *grlc*: it assumes that SPARQL queries can (and should) be uniquely and globally identifiable on the Web through URIs, for example http://mydomain.org/myqueries/query1.sparql; just as Linked Data and RDF propose to identify any Web resource, so this should apply to queries as well. *Because* SPARQL queries acquire this "full Web citizenship," services can retrieve and operate on them as they need; in *grlc*'s case, to automatically build Web APIs using them. Circumstantially, most of this chapter also assumes GitHub as this HTTP server and URI manager (because any file stored in GitHub acquires these features automatically); but, again, this is not required and any other alternative providing similar features will work just fine.

By leveraging these principles, *grlc* can automatically create Web APIs on top of SPARQL endpoints **with zero coding**, practically and effectively supporting developers to deploy Web APIs for Knowledge Graphs in no time, saving resources, and helping them focus on other, more critical Knowledge Graph architecture parts.

grlc is written in Python. Its source code is available at https://github.com/CLARIAH/grlc under the permissive MIT license. It can be installed via Python package manager "pip" available at https://pypi.org/project/grlc/. A docker image is also available: https://hub.docker.com/r/clariah/grlc. A permanent instance of *grlc* service is available at https://grlc.io/.

---

[1] https://github.com
[2] This just means that a HTTP server will respond to HTTP requests to the URIs representing SPARQL queries with their actual content.

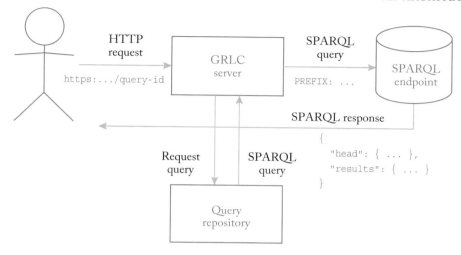

Figure 4.1: Diagram of *grlc* architecture.

4.2   ARCHITECTURE

grlc is based on a very simple architecture. It consists of an HTTP server, which accepts HTTP requests from a client. The URL of these requests is mapped to a SPARQL query stored in a query repository. This query repository can be Github, the local storage or a remote location available via HTTP. When the SPARQL query has been resolved based on the HTTP request, the query can be executed in a SPARQL endpoint. Results from the SPARQL query are returned to the user as an HTTP response to the original request. Figure 4.1 illustrates this architecture.

Within this architecture, *grlc* supports and can carry on the following two use-cases, illustrated in Figure 4.2.

1. The generation of valid and complete Open API-based (see Chapter 3) API specifications; and the generation of UIs and documentation of such API specifications based on the Swagger UI.[3]

2. The actual *execution* of the operations indicated in such API specifications.

Open API-based specifications and UIs   This is shown at the top flow in Figure 4.2. Through this service, a client can request either the Open API specification of a SPARQL query collection stored in an external query management repository (e.g., GitHub) in JSON; or the equivalent Swagger UI built on top of such specification. In both cases, *grlc* makes various requests to the external query management system, retrieving the query collection metadata (such as the name, license, and creator of the query collection) and also the contents of the specific queries in such collection. Those queries are **annotated with YAML**, as we will see later in this chapter, to fully describe how the query should

[3]https://swagger.io/tools/swagger-ui/

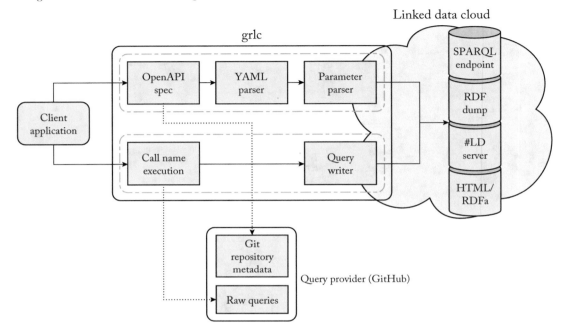

Figure 4.2: *grlc*'s basic features: generation of API specifications (top path) and execution of API operations (bottom path)—with its interaction with external systems.

be interpreted in the context of a Web API (for example, a summary of what the query does and the address of the SPARQL endpoint against which it is meant to be executed). A YAML parser deals with those annotations, and together with a parameter parser they put together a valid and complete Open API specification that is finally returned to the client.

Operation/callname execution   This is shown at the bottom flow in Figure 4.2. Through this service, a client can request to directly execute one of the operations listed in the Open API specification. When this is invoked, *grlc* makes requests to the actual contents of the query from the query management system; retrieving, again, its body (the SPARQL syntax) and the YAML annotations. With these, *grlc* can map any passed HTTP parameter to its query rewriter, which replaces certain variables, as we will see later, with the value of those HTTP parameters. Finally, *grlc* sends the SPARQL query to the SPARQL endpoint indicated in the YAML metadata via HTTP, obtains its results, and returns them to the client in the requested format.

The public instance of *grlc* at https://grlc.io/ is useful here to show how the *grlc*'s API implements these two services/use cases. Assuming that the query management system *grlc* uses is GitHub, and that such system exposes SPARQL queries at https://github.com/:owner/:repo, where :`owner` is a username and :`repo` is a repository name, then:

- https://grlc.io/api-git/:owner/:repo/spec returns the query collection Open API specification in JSON.

- https://grlc.io/api-git/:owner/:repo/ returns the full-blown, Swagger UI based on such specification.

- https://grlc.io/api-git/:owner/:repo/:operation?p_1=v_1...p_n=v_n calls the operation/query named :operation with the indicated parameter values.

Nevertheless, GitHub is not the only query management system supported. The following routes are also available via alternative APIs:

- https://grlc.io/api-local/ for queries stored locally.

- https://grlc.io/api-url/ for queries published elsewhere on the Web via any standard HTTP server.[4]

The next Section illustrates the use of all these services and use cases with practical examples.

4.3   WORKING WITH *grlc*

The aim of a Knowledge Graph API is to allow end users to explore a Knowledge Graph. Depending on who the intended user is, their level of technical expertise may vary. In order to maximize the number of users who can access the data using an API, it should require as little specialized technical knowledge as possible. In this way users do not need to worry about the syntax to access the data they are interested in, and can focus in what the data means to them.

Let's assume a user is interested in exploring the information available on DBpedia related to music bands. DBpedia contains a long collection of music bands, with related information of the genre of music the band is associated with, and the albums the band has produced. Our user should be able to access this information by using an API which can directly give her/him this information.

If our user is familiar with SPARQL, she/he could use a SPARQL query in the DBpedia endpoint https://dbpedia.org/sparql and use a query like the following:

```
PREFIX rdf: <http://www.w3.org/1999/02/22-rdf-syntax-ns#>
PREFIX dbo: <http://dbpedia.org/ontology/>
PREFIX schema: <http://schema.org/>

SELECT ?band ?album ?genre WHERE {
  ?band rdf:type dbo:Band .
  ?album rdf:type schema:MusicAlbum .
```

---

[4]Collections supplied in this fashion need to comply with a concrete specification; see https://github.com/CLARIAH/grlc/blob/master/README.md.

```
    ?band dbo:genre ?genre .
    ?album dbo:artist ?band .
} LIMIT 100
```

Listing 4.1: Querying list of band, album, and genre from DBpedia.

However, if she/he is not familiar with SPARQL—or does not want to bother with SPARQL syntax every time there is need to look at this data—she/he could create this query once (potentially with help of a SPARQL-saavy colleague), store this query in Github (for example https://github.com/ CLARIAH/grlc-queries/blob/master/description.rq) and use *grlc* to execute this query, by simply visiting the URL https://grlc.io/api-git/CLARIAH/grlc-queries/description.

This page would produce a result similar to this:

```
"band","album","genre"
"http://dbpedia.org/resource/Asia_(band)","http://dbpedia.org/resource/Axioms_(album)
    ","http://dbpedia.org/resource/Art_rock"
"http://dbpedia.org/resource/Asia_(band)","http://dbpedia.org/resource/Axioms_(album)
    ","http://dbpedia.org/resource/Progressive_rock"
"http://dbpedia.org/resource/Asia_(band)","http://dbpedia.org/resource/Axioms_(album)
    ","http://dbpedia.org/resource/Album-oriented_rock"
"http://dbpedia.org/resource/Asia_(band)","http://dbpedia.org/resource/Axioms_(album)
    ","http://dbpedia.org/resource/Arena_rock"
"http://dbpedia.org/resource/Bauhaus_(band)","http://dbpedia.org/resource/
    Swing_the_Heartache:_The_BBC_Sessions","http://dbpedia.org/resource/Gothic_rock"
"http://dbpedia.org/resource/Bauhaus_(band)","http://dbpedia.org/resource/
    Swing_the_Heartache:_The_BBC_Sessions","http://dbpedia.org/resource/Post-punk"
"http://dbpedia.org/resource/Catatonia_(band)","http://dbpedia.org/resource/
    Paper_Scissors_Stone_(album)","http://dbpedia.org/resource/Alternative_rock"
```

Listing 4.2: Results from query in Listing 4.1.

Executing such a query works for accessing a specific piece of information, but it is not very flexible and it would produce a very long list of results. Our user may want to access information only information from rock bands, in which case the query is modified in:

```
PREFIX rdf: <http://www.w3.org/1999/02/22-rdf-syntax-ns#>
PREFIX dbo: <http://dbpedia.org/ontology/>
PREFIX schema: <http://schema.org/>

SELECT ?band ?album WHERE {
  ?band rdf:type dbo:Band .
  ?album rdf:type schema:MusicAlbum .
  ?band dbo:genre <http://dbpedia.org/resource/Rock_music> .
```

```
  ?album dbo:artist ?band .
} LIMIT 100
```

Listing 4.3: Querying list of rock bands and albums from DBpedia.

The next day she/he might be interested in looking at alternative rock bands, and yet again a different query would be generated:

```
PREFIX rdf: <http://www.w3.org/1999/02/22-rdf-syntax-ns#>
PREFIX dbo: <http://dbpedia.org/ontology/>
PREFIX schema: <http://schema.org/>

SELECT ?band ?album WHERE {
  ?band rdf:type dbo:Band .
  ?album rdf:type schema:MusicAlbum .
  ?band dbo:genre
          <http://dbpedia.org/resource/Alternative_rock> .
  ?album dbo:artist ?band .
} LIMIT 100
```

Listing 4.4: Querying list of alternative bands and albums from DBpedia.

Clearly this does not scale. *grlc* provides a parameter mapping mechanism which allows a query to define a variable which gets replaced by an API parameter. For example, our user could use the query in Listing 4.5.

```
PREFIX rdf: <http://www.w3.org/1999/02/22-rdf-syntax-ns#>
PREFIX dbo: <http://dbpedia.org/ontology/>
PREFIX schema: <http://schema.org/>

SELECT ?band ?album WHERE {
  ?band rdf:type dbo:Band .
  ?album rdf:type schema:MusicAlbum .
  ?band dbo:genre ?_genre_iri .
  ?album dbo:artist ?band .
} LIMIT 100
```

Listing 4.5: Querying list of bands and albums from DBpedia from a specified genre.

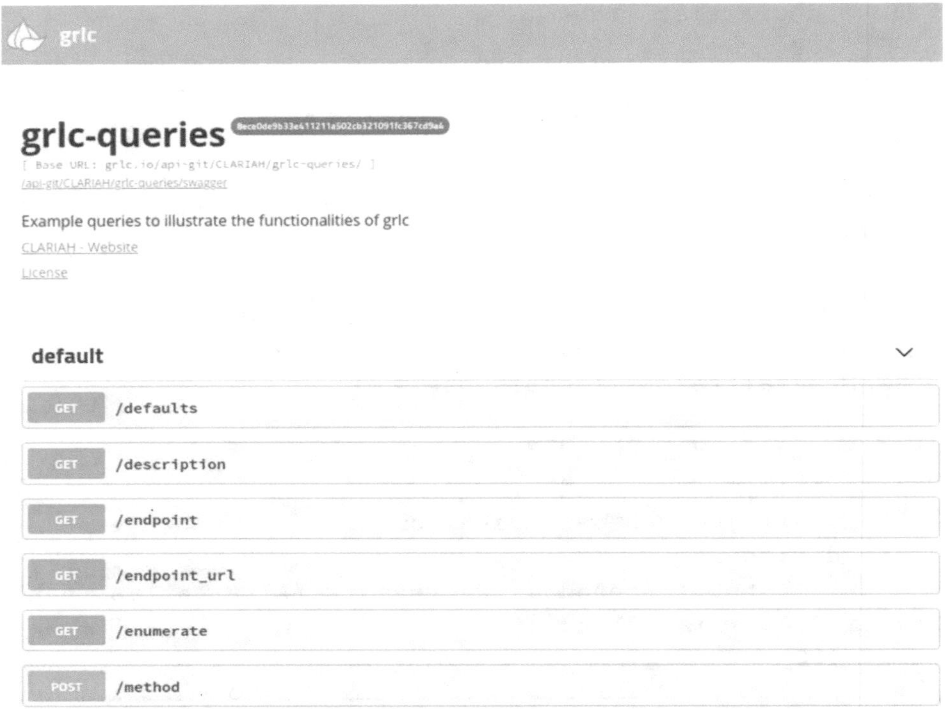

Figure 4.3: Auto-generated OpenAPI documentation.

This query includes the special variable *?_genre_iri* which when executing the query via the API will turn into the URL parameter *genre*.[5] Our user could then use different two differ-ent URLs: http://grlc.io/api-git/CLARIAH/grlc-queries/enumerate?genre=http://dbpedia.org/resource/ Rock_music for rock or http://grlc.io/api-git/CLARIAH/grlc-queries/enumerate?genre=http://dbpedia. org/resource/Alternative_rock for alternative rock—or replace the *genre* parameter with any other genre.

In web API development, it is usual to use tools for API documentation such as the OpenAPI specification (Section 3.1.1). *grlc* makes use of OpenAPI to generate API documentation. For *grlc* APIs, the OpenAPI definition allows the user to understand which queries are available to access a Knowledge Graph, representing those in a web page (Figure 4.3. Going back to our earlier example, our user would be able inspect the Swagger API specification of her/his queries by visiting: http://grlc. io/api-git/CLARIAH/grlc-queries.

---

[5]More details about variables are reported in Section 4.4.2.

4.4   FEATURES

Web APIs are more powerful when they provide sufficient flexibility to enable consumers to use access data in an optimal way. *grlc* accommodates for flexible APIs by means of query *decorators* and variable mapping.

Decorators are special keywords included at the top of the file containing a SPARQL query. They provide special functionality, feeding the OpenAPI documentation generated by *grlc* (Section 4.4.1), adding variable parameters to API endpoints (Section 4.4.2), modifying how queries are executed (Section 4.4.3), and manipulating query responses (Section 4.4.4). All decorators start with #+, for example:

```
#+ decorator_1: value_1
#+ decorator_2: value_2
```

Listing 4.6: Query decorator syntax example.

In the next sections we describe the different decorators that can be used.

4.4.1   QUERY DOCUMENTATION

There are three decorators which can be used to document *grlc* generated APIs. These decorators modify the documentation UI but have no further effect.

- summary – Creates a summary of your query/operation. This is shown next to your operation name in the documentation.

- description – Creates a description of your query/operation. This is shown as the description of your operation in the documentation. The description can be longer than a summary as there is more space in the documentation to display the description.

- tags – OpenAPI allows for queries to be grouped together. Each query/operation can be assigned a tag. Queries/operations with the same tag will be part of the same group. This allows users to organize their queries/operations.

4.4.2   QUERY VARIABLES

The next group of decorators can modify how query variables are handled in the documentation UI. Before describing these decorators, we should describe the function and syntax of query variables in *grlc*.

Queries can be made more flexible by dynamically replacing variables in the query. This is called parameter mapping, because HTTP parameters are mapped to these query variables. In *grlc*, a variable is defined by adding _ to a SPARQL variable, like this: ?_var. By default, variables will be replaced by literals. Other data types are supported and can be indicated by appending an additional _ for example:

- `?_name_en` will be interpreted as a literal written in English; this can be done with any language tag.

- `?_name_integer` will be interpreted as an integer.

- `?_name_iri` will be interpreted as an IRI.

- `?_name_prefix_datatype` will be interpreted as a datatype of type `^^prefix:datatype`.

If we want to allow that a variable may have no replacement, two underscores (`?__name`) can be used to create an optional parameter.

Additionally, there are decorators which affect how query variables appear in the documentation UI:

- `defaults` – sets a default value in the documentation. This value can be changed, so it serves mostly as a hint to the user.

- `enumerate` – creates a dropdown menu in the documentation, listing possible values for the variable.

4.4.3   QUERY EXECUTION

The next group of decorators affects how queries are routed by the *grlc* server and executed by an underlying SPARQL endpoint.

- `method` – indicates the HTTP request method (`GET` or `POST`) used to communicate with the *grlc* server. `GET` is the default.

- `endpoint` – specifies a default SPARQL endpoint for the query execution. This provides the flexibility for the same query to be executed on different SPARQL endpoints, by changing the default value in the UI or in the HTTP query parameters.

- `endpoint_in_url` – enables or disables the possibility to use the `endpoint` parameter. This can be used to restrict the use of a specific SPARQL endpoint to execute queries.

4.4.4   QUERY RESULT MANIPULATION

The final group of decorators affects how the results from the SPARQL query are sent back from the server. This is useful to provide the client application calling the API with a convenient way to work with the query results.

- `pagination` – paginates the results in groups of (for example) 100. This allows the client application to handle smaller volumes of data per API call.

- `transform` – allows query results to be converted to the specified JSON structure, by using SPARQLTransformer. See Section 5.4 for more details.

4.5   EXERCISES

This section provides a series of exercises which aim at providing practical experience of turning a SPARQL query into a web API using *grlc*.

You can test your solution using https://grlc.io/, by reading your queries from a GitHub repository,[6] or from a specification file.[7] You can also run your own copy of *grlc* and load your queries from your local file system.[8] All solutions are in Appendix A.

Exercise 4.1 Create an API that retrieves all bands from DBpedia.
  Tip: Use the DBpedia ontology type `dbo:Band`.

Exercise 4.2 Create an API that lists bands that play either Rock or Jazz, and that have either Liverpool or Los Angeles as hometown.
  Tip 1: Use the DBPedia ontology types `dbo:genre` and `dbo:hometown`.
  Tip 2: Use the *grlc* enumerate decorator.

Exercise 4.3 Expand the API from the previous exercise by adding documentation and making sure your query can only be run on DBpedia SPARQL endpoint.
  Tip: Use the `summary`, `description`, `endpoint`, and `endpoint_in_url` decorators.

Exercise 4.4 Create an API that lists the name, genre and hometown of bands whose name matches a given string.
  Tip 1: Use the DBpedia property type *dbp:name*.
  Tip 2: Because DBpedia uses Virtuoso, you can use the built in function *bif:contains*.[9]

---

[6]https://github.com/CLARIAH/grlc#from-a-github-repository
[7]https://github.com/CLARIAH/grlc#specification-file-syntax
[8]https://github.com/CLARIAH/grlc#from-local-storage
[9]http://docs.openlinksw.com/virtuoso/rdfsparqlrulefulltext/

CHAPTER 5

Shaping JSON Results: *SPARQL Transformer*

When interacting with Knowledge Graphs, applications deal with two complementary items: data requests and data responses. So far, we have discussed the first item, but this chapter focuses instead on the data response. We point out the limitations of standard formats and identify development needs, proposing a technological solution.

5.1 SPARQL RESULTS JSON FORMAT: THE CURSE OF THE BINDINGS

Many Knowledge Graphs store data following the RDF data model. The connections between subjects and objects build a graph structure of nodes and edges. On the Web, JavaScript is the undisputed leading language, while the JSON format is the de-facto standard for data serialization. In contrast with the RDF graph, the structure of a JSON document is more similar to a tree, with objects nested inside others. As a consequence, the RDF data model has to be converted somehow from a graph to a tree for enabling consumption by web applications. This kind of tree structure is also common in other programming languages. As examples, we can mention dictionaries in Python and hashes in Ruby. We can state that this issue goes beyond the web development context and is crucial for all applications consuming RDF data. Hence, we need to understand how to move from RDF to JSON and, in particular, what will be the final structure. Significant literature tackles this problem from different perspectives [Barton, 2004, Broekstra et al., 2002].

As seen in Chapter 1, JSON-LD is a standard RDF serialization. JSON-LD is a valid JSON document—therefore, fully compatible with JavaScript—enhanced with special key properties for mapping properties to URIs (`@context`), carrying the RDF data (`@graph`), referencing the RDF identifier (`@id`) and type (`@type`) of any object. We might conclude that JSON-LD is the solution to our dilemma, if not for one detail that we cannot ignore. **JSON-LD is not a graph**. We can convert it into a (RDF) graph in a deterministic manner. Nonetheless, its shape is definitively a tree, and cannot be otherwise, since JSON-LD is a valid JSON.

Further evidence is that an RDF graph can be represented by more than one different JSON-LD document. Let's take as an example a graph about film metadata, in which each film node is directly connected to the nodes representing actors and directors (Figure 5.1). If we want to convert this graph into JSON-LD, we have a choice. Where do we start? From which root node do we start building our tree? In our case, we have at least three possible choices. We can represent this data as an array of

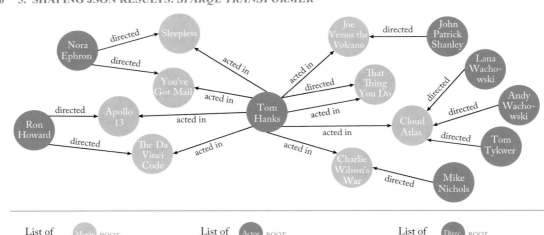

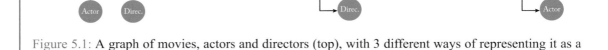

Figure 5.1: A graph of movies, actors and directors (top), with 3 different ways of representing it as a tree (bottom).

films, each of them containing information about the actors and directors involved. Or, we can have the actors at the top, grouping together for each of them the set of films in which they performed—with their respective directors. Or, finally, we can do the same work by choosing the directors as root, then on a second level the films, finally the actors. This choice certainly depends on our ultimate goal, i.e., how we want to use this data. However, you should take into account that this choice is not trivial and software and DBMS do not make it for you.

If you have some experience with SPARQL endpoints, you also know that the JSON output of a query is not JSON-LD.[1] When performing a SELECT query, the standard structure follows a W3C recommendation called **SPARQL Query Result JSON Format**.[2] This structure is made of two members:

- the head object contains some metadata, such as the list of variable names used in the results; and

- the results object has a required key (bindings) containing the query results. It may also include other kinds of metadata, such as if results are ordered.

We give now a better look to the bindings key, which is a list of results objects as binding of variables. This means that each object represents a single query solution; its keys are query variable

---

[1] Exceptions are some kinds of queries, such as DESCRIBE, that output RDF data as results, and for which endpoints (e.g., Virtuoso) offer JSON-LD output.

[2] SPARQL Query Result JSON Format recommendation https://www.w3.org/TR/sparql11-results-json/.

names and its values are JSON objects containing always a `type` (uri, literal or blank node) and a `value` represented as a string, sometimes a `datatype` or a `xml:lang` tag. With this structure, reading any value from the results means accessing 2 objects keys (`results` and `bindings`), then an array item, then again 2 keys (the involved variable and `value`), for a total of 5 levels, deeper in the structure than what a developer may expect.

As the query results represent all the valid solutions of the query, it is possible that two bindings differ only by a single field. We can take the query in Listing 4.1 as an example and run it against DBpedia. Looking at the results in any format (JSON included), we can see several repetitions in the band values: each band appears in the results $N * M$ times, where N is the number of albums by the band and M the genres assigned to it. The more variables there are, the more repetitions are possible. From another perspective, it is as if we are reading tabular data; each line is a solution and each cell contains (maximum) a value. This is confirmed by looking at the query results in Listing 4.2: in the first 7 bindings, *Asia (band)* appears 4 times (1 album * 4 genres), while *Bauhaus (band)* appears 2 times (1 album * 2 genres). For obtaining complete information about a specific band, we need to collect all related bindings. In the worst scenario, pagination may split these bindings into different pages, hampering the collection task.

Having described the standard JSON format, several barriers obstruct the data consumption from a web development perspective. In particular, developers have to accomplish four recurrent tasks.

1. **Skip redundant metadata.** Often, the metadata in the SPARQL output is simply not used by developers. For example, this is true for the list of used variables names in the `head` object: not only it is already known from the query, but one might also infer it directly from the results. In practice, developers may ignore completely this part and check for the availability of a certain property directly in the bindings.

2. **Reducing and parsing.** The value of a property is always wrapped in an object with the *type* and *value* attributes. All literals are returned as strings, without regard to the original RDF datatype, expressed separately. A simpler structure can be obtained by extracting the final value from its wrapping object and directly attach it to the variable key, taking care of the casting of numbers and Booleans.

3. **Merging.** The repetition of values is one of the biggest limitations of bindings. Merging them based on common URIs is therefore crucial. Nevertheless, we need to make a choice about which node will be the root of the merged tree and the anchor for the merging. The developer needs to be in charge of this choice, and technology must empower her/him in this task.

4. **Mapping.** There may exist specific needs for giving the results a particular structure or vocabulary, i.e., for using the data in input to a third-party library, or for embedding metadata in web pages following *schema.org*.

The libraries seen in Section 2.2 solve one or more of these problems, but none of them handle all. In particular, the merging of results is unusually taken in charge, leaving the developer alone against the curse of the bindings.

5.2   DATA RESHAPE WITH *SPARQL TRANSFORMER*

```
[
  {
    "id": "http://dbpedia.org/resource/Asia_(band)",
    "album": "http://dbpedia.org/resource/Axioms_(album)",
    "genre": [
      "http://dbpedia.org/resource/Art_rock",
      "http://dbpedia.org/resource/Progressive_rock",
      "http://dbpedia.org/resource/Album-oriented_rock",
      "http://dbpedia.org/resource/Arena_rock"
    ]
  },
  {
    "id": "http://dbpedia.org/resource/Bauhaus_(band)",
    "album": "http://dbpedia.org/resource/Swing_the_Heart...",
    "genre": [
      "http://dbpedia.org/resource/Gothic_rock",
      "http://dbpedia.org/resource/Post-punk"
    ]
  },
  ...
```

Listing 5.1: Result from query in Listing 4.1 obtained with *SPARQL Transformer*.

The goal of avoiding the above-introduced recurrent tasks is at the foundation of a different method for writing and executing queries. *SPARQL Transformer* (ST) [Lisena and Troncy, 2018, Lisena et al., 2019] is an approach for accessing data contained in SPARQL repositories and obtaining them in a convenient JSON shape. It consists of two main components: (1) a JSON-based query syntax and (2) a library that processes this syntax and uses it for retrieving data.

With ST, it is possible to obtain a result similar to the one in Listing 5.1: each band is represented using a single object, collecting all its albums and genres in a single array. This can be obtained thanks to the merging capabilities of ST, driven by user choices. In addition, this output does not include

Prototype definition
- describe the template
- define the replacements
- options and filters

\$-Modifiers

\$where \$values \$limit \$distinct
\$orderly \$groupby \$filter ...

```
{
  "proto": {
    "id"    : "?band",
    "album" : "?album",
    "genre" : "$dbo:genre$required"
  },
  "$where" : [
    "?band a dbo:Band",
    "?album a schema:MusicAlbum",
    "?album dbo:artist ?band"
  ],
  "$limit": 100
}
```

Figure 5.2: An example of JSON Query, in which it is possible to distinguish the prototype definition and the \$-modifiers.

unnecessary metadata. Among other features, Booleans and numbers are automatically parsed and you can easily define and change the requested language for literals in localized queries.

5.2.1   A SINGLE JSON OBJECT AS QUERY AND TEMPLATE

The core of ST is the use of a single JSON object, called *JSON query*, for describing at the same time how to find the information (the query) and which structure is required in output (the desired template).[3] This object is composed of two parts: the prototype definition and a set of \$-modifiers. Figure 5.2 show the transposition of Listing 4.1 into the ST syntax.

The **prototype definition** is introduced by the `proto` keyword. The structure of the prototype will be reflected by each object in the final results, so that it can be modified in order to match the desired output format. The leaf nodes—the literal property values—will be replaced by incoming data according to specific rules. In particular:

1. **variable nodes**, which start with a question mark "?" (like ?band), will be replaced by the value of the homonym SPARQL variable;

2. **predicate nodes**, which starts with a "\$" sign (like \$dbo:genre), will be replaced by the object of a specific RDF triple; and

3. **literal nodes**, which cover all the eventual other contents, are not replaced and will be preserved in the output, regardless of the query results.

[3]The use of a single object put *SPARQL Transformer* at a certain distance also from SPARQL CONSTRUCT, in which the query and the final structure are two distinct parts of the query.

Together with the prototype definition, the query object contains a number of **$-modifiers** which give access to specific SPARQL features, such as $where and $limit. **Inline $-modifiers** can appear also in the prototype leaf nodes, modifying the standard behavior of that field (e.g., $required).

In the results, literals are automatically parsed into the suitable type: string, boolean, or number (further distinguished into integer and float in Python). This conversion is done relying on the original datatype information. Dates and times are excluded from the automatic parsing and preserved as strings; this keeps the final results compatible with the JSON standard—which does not define date-time types—leaving eventual parsing to the user. The information about the language is preserved wrapping the literals in an intermediate object inspired by JSON-LD. This object separates the language tag and the value in two different fields, according to the following structure:

```
{
  "language": "en",
  "value" : "Asia (band)"
}
```

Listing 5.2: A leaf node in the results with the preserved language tag.

5.2.2   ARCHITECTURE

The **SPARQL Transformer library**, compliant with the so-described syntax, is available in two different open-source implementations:

- in JavaScript[4] published on NPM.[5] This version offers the library as an ECMAScript Module, designed to both work in Node.js and the browser; and

- in Python,[6] published on PyPI.[7] This version returns a dict object, which can be directly manipulated by the code—in scripts or notebooks—and it is particularly recommended in research applications. In addition, the output can be serialized in JSON using standard Python methods, for example to serve it in web applications using Flask or Django.

Both versions present an architecture as in Figure 5.3. The input of the library is a JSON query, following the syntax seen before. A *Parser* component reads the input and extracts (1) a SPARQL SELECT query and (2) a clean version of the prototype, in which each JSON key is assigned a placeholder SPARQL variable. This variable can be defined by the user or automatically generated by the library. The SPARQL query is then passed to the *Query Performer*, in charge of performing the request to the SPARQL endpoint and returning the results in the JSON standard JSON format. Finally, the *Shaper*

---

[4]https://github.com/D2KLab/sparql-transformer
[5]https://www.npmjs.com/package/sparql-transformer
[6]https://github.com/D2KLab/py-sparql-transformer
[7]https://pypi.org/project/SPARQLTransformer/

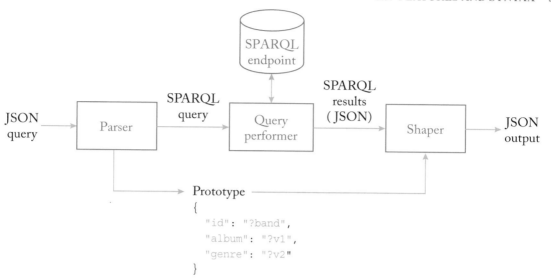

Figure 5.3: Architecture of *SPARQL Transformer*.

accesses the results and reshapes each binding into the prototype template, leveraging the placeholders for inserting the values in the right place. In addition, data-type parsing, pruning of nodes with no value (from OPTIONAL blocks), and merging of the objects with common identifiers are applied.

Given that its interactions consist of SPARQL queries and HTTP requests, *SPARQL Transformer* is compatible with any SPARQL endpoint by specifying its public address. It can be used as middleware between the endpoint and the application, as an alternative to or in combination with other SPARQL clients (Chapter 2). The Query Performer can be replaced by the user with a custom one, for fulfilling different requirements for accessing the endpoint (e.g., authentication) or for integration into more complex environments.

5.3   FEATURES AND SYNTAX

After giving an overview of *SPARQL Transformer* in the previous section, we are going to explore in deep the capabilities of the library. Also, the JSON query syntax will be detailed, providing a comprehensive tutorial.

SPARQL Transformer also accept an alternative syntax, based on **JSON-LD**. This syntax only modifies some keywords to better reflect the standard JSON-LD syntax, as reported in Table 5.1. It can be used to shape the results according to a vocabulary such as schema.org, providing a proper @context. Please note that @type[8] has no special behavior in *SPARQL Transformer* and its value is preserved in output as a literal node.

---

[8] @type is a standard JSON-LD keyword used for expressing the RDF class of the described entity

Table 5.1: Differences in keywords between the two alternative *SPARQL Transformer* syntaxes which may be found in the context of the query or of the final results

Context	JSON Syntax	JSON-LD Syntax
query	`proto`	`@graph`
	`id`	`@id`
results	`language`	`@language`
	`value`	`@value`

The library automatically detects the used syntax and processes the JSON query accordingly. The remainder of the chapter will use the JSON syntax, even if the same features are available for the two variants.

5.3.1   MERGING AROUND AN ANCHOR

In Section 5.1, we have discussed the complexity of choosing the element at the root of the JSON tree. *SPARQL Transformer* allows the user to select this root through keywords and modifiers in the JSON query syntax. We define here the concept of **anchor**, a variable in the prototype with a dual role. First, it is the subject of all the sibling predicate nodes. Second, it acts as the core of the merging strategy.

By default, the anchor is the `id` property. This is what happens in Figure 5.2. The `?band` variable is chosen as the subject of `dbo:genre`, resulting in:

```
?band dbo:genre ?v1
```

where the object variable `?v1` is automatically assigned. In the results (Listing 5.1), the bindings with the same `id` value are aggregated into a single object, while the others appear as arrays.

The merging is applied at different levels of the JSON tree. Figure 5.4 extends the query about bands with the addition of the band name and the genre label, introducing a second level (the `genre` object) in the JSON tree. You can notice the automatically generated variables `?v1`, `?v2`, and `?v3`. Each level has its own `id`, which serves as the subject for the sibling predicate nodes. In this way, the subject for the first `rdfs:label` is `?band`, while it is `?v2` for the second one. The node `genre.id` is a predicate node with the role of anchor, which is handled as a special case: not having a sibling anchor node—apart from itself—its subject is the parent anchor, in this case `?band`. Given this kind of query, the aggregation of results is performed as follows. First, the bindings are merged on the root `id`. Those having the same value for `?band` are grouped and represented as a single object. In this object, sibling predicate nodes (`name` and `album`) are expressed as an array of distinct values. Finally, all nested objects are merged on their own anchor. Looking again at our example, for each band, the `genre` objects with the same `genre.id` are merged. In this way, the final output contains one object

```
{                                       SELECT DISTINCT ?band ?album ?v1 ?v2 ?v3
  "proto" : {                           WHERE {
    "id"    : "?band",
    "name"   : "$rdfs:label$required",      ?band rdfs:label ?v1 .
    "album" : "?album",
    "genre" : {
      "id"    : "$dbo:genre$required",      ?band dbo:genre ?v2 .
      "label": "$rdfs:label$required" }     ?v2 rdfs:label ?v3 .
  },
  "$where": [
      "?band a dbo:Band",                   ?band a dbo:Band .
      "?album a schema:MusicAlbum",         ?album a schema:MusicAlbum .
      "?album dbo:artist ?band"             ?album dbo:artist ?band.
  ],                                    }
  "$limit": 100                         LIMIT 100
}
```

Figure 5.4: A JSON query for retrieving the list of music bands, with labels, albums, and genres. On the right, the equivalent SPARQL query. The arrows mark the transformation from a line in the JSON query to a line in the SPARQL query.

for each band, including on its own all distinct labels, albums and genres. A genre is represented only once for each band, with all its different labels.

Is the use of an id keyword mandatory for enabling the merging? Development needs may require a different naming convention or a structure not including an id property. In those cases, it is possible to select an alternative anchor by appending to the JSON value the inline modifier $anchor. For instance, we may change Figure 5.4 in order to store the band URI in a band property, replacing line 3 ("id": "?band") with:

```
    "band": "?band$anchor"
```

While the resulting SPARQL query remains unchanged, the prototype avoids the id keyword and allows the user to select a different anchor.[9] The latter inherits the role of subject for SPARQL predicates and the one of merging nodes. If both are present, the $anchor modifier takes priority over the id keyword; in other words, the $anchor modifier allows to have a id property in the final JSON structure without any special role in the query process.

[9]Likewise, the genre's id may have been replaced with "genre_id":"$dbo:genre$required$anchor".

5.3.2   OVERVIEW OF $-MODIFIERS

The $-modifiers mimic SPARQL features in the JSON query syntax. When defined in the root of the JSON query—outside the prototype definition—they apply to the whole query. All root $-modifier requires an input expressed as JSON value of the property.

As already seen in Figure 5.2, $where is used for writing WHERE clauses in plain SPARQL. $where accepts as input a string or an array of strings, similarly to $orderby, $groupby, $having, and $filter, each one replicating the homonym SPARQL feature. It is possible to limit the query results using $limit, eventually combining it with $offset for implementing a pagination of results. This limit can be performed in two alternative modalities, controlled by the value of the $limitMode modifier:

- query: the results are limited using the LIMIT/OFFSET standard SPARQL keyword, by the SPARQL endpoint itself. This means that the limit is applied on raw bindings, and the number of merged objects can vary; and

- library: the results are limited after transformation. This ensures that the number of objects in the output is exactly equal to the value of $limit, with a possible increment in query execution time due to the retrieval of all results from the endpoint.

By default, *SPARQL Transformer* retrieves unique results by including the DISTINCT keyword in the SPARQL query; it is anyway possible to disable this behavior setting "$distinct": false. It is possible to declare the mapping between a prefix and a URI using a key-value pair of the JSON object as input to the $prefixes modifier. Similarly, $values allows to define the possible values of a variable—relying on the VALUES feature of SPARQL—using key-value pairs; this modifier can be used to include parameters in queries and dynamically change their values from your code. The nodes impacted by $values definitions are automatically marked as required. The full list of root $-modifiers is included in Table 5.2.

Inline $-modifiers are declared in the prototype, appended at the end of the object values (leaf nodes), regardless of their being variable or predicate nodes. Their effect applies to the element in which they are defined. Each node can have one or more inline modifiers resulting in a set of $-separated elements.

Some modifiers may accept an input, declared immediately after the modifier and introduced by a colon. This input can be required or optional. In particular, the $var modifier requires a string input (ex. $var:name) to be used as object variable instead of an automatically generated one. This is useful for reusing that variable in other modifiers, like $filter or $values. The full list of inline $-modifiers is included in Table 5.3.

5.3.3   DEALING WITH LANGUAGES

The presence of labels in different languages is one of the reasons for value repetition in bindings. In RDF, literals can be represented together with a language tag, like in "Asia (band)"@en or "Asia

Table 5.2: Full list of root $-modifiers

Modifier	Input	Note
$where	string, array	Add where clause in the triple format. Ex. "$where": "?id a dbo:City"
$values	object	Set VALUES for specified variables as a map. The presence of a lang tag or of the $lang attribute attached to the related property is taken into account. Ex. "$values": {"?id": ["dbr:Paris", "http://dbpedia.org/resource/Roma"]}
$limit	number	LIMIT the SPARQL results
$limitMode	"query" (default) or "library"	Perform the LIMIT operation in the query or on the obtained results (library)
$offset	number	OFFSET applied to the SPARQL results
$from	string(uri)	Define the graph FROM which selecting the results
$distinct	boolean (default true)	Set the DISTINCT in the select
$orderby	string, array	Build an ORDER BY on the variables in the input. Ex. "$orderby":["DESC(?name)","?age"]
$groupby	string, array	Build an GROUP BY on the variables in the input. Ex. "$groupby":"?id"
$having	string, array	Allows to declare the content of HAVING. If it is an array, the items are concatenated by &&.
$filter	string, array	Add the content as a FILTER. Ex. "$filter": "?myNum >3"
$prefixes	object	Set the prefixes in the format: "foaf": "http://xmlns.com/foaf/0.1/".
$lang	:acceptedLangs[string]	The default language to use as $bestlang (see Table 5.3), expressed through the Accept-Language standard. Ex. $lang:en;q=1, it;q=0.7 *;q=0.1
$langTag	"hide", "show" (default)	When hide, language tags are not included in the output. Ex. hide → "label":"Bologna"; show → "label":{"value": "Bologna", "language": "it"}

Table 5.3: Full list of inline $-modifiers. All options are required unless differently specified.

Modifier	Input	Note
$required	n/a	When omitted, the clause is wrapped by OPTIONAL { ... }.
$sample	n/a	Extract a single value for that property by adding a SAMPLE(?v) in the SELECT.
$lang	:lang [string, optional]	FILTER by language. In absence of a language, pick the first value of $lang in the root. Ex. $lang:it, $lang:en, $lang.
$bestlang	:acceptedLangs [string, optional]	Choose the best match (using BEST_LANGMATCH) over the languages according to the list expressed through the Accept-Language standard. This list can be declared as option or expressed as $lang in the root. Ex. $bestlang, $bestlang:en, or $bestlang:en;q=1,it;q=0.7 *;q=0.1
$var	:var[string]	Specify the variable that will be assigned in the query, so that it can be referred in the root properties (like $filter). If missing, a ? is prepended. Ex. $var:myVariable, $var:?name
$anchor	n/a	Set this property as merging anchor. The set is valid for the current level in the JSON tree, ignoring eventual id/@id sibling properties. Ex. Having "myprop":"?example$anchor", ?example is the subject of SPARQL statements and the final results are merged on myprop.
$reverse	n/a	Set this property for use the current variable as subject of the SPARQL predicate, rather than object.
$count $sum $min $max $avg	n/a	Return the respective aggregate function (COUNT, SUM, MIN, MAX, AVG) on the variable.

(groupe)"@fr. SPARQL queries return indeed all available labels, regardless of the specified language tag. Features like FILTER can be used to restrict the result set to those with the preferred language.

Multilingual labels can be handled in different ways, depending on the desired objective. A web application for a museum archive may need to display the information in both English and the original language of a painting, with appropriate language tags. If instead we want to expose pharmaceutical data from a specialized KG, we would choose to show the information about drugs in a single language, possibly selected by the user. When the selected language is missing, it would be nice to have a fallback solution, like displaying the English label.

The language selection can be controlled by two different inline modifiers. $lang allows to filter the result according to a given language, resulting in a SPARQL FILTER. For example, by setting $lang:en only literals marked as English will be returned. Using instead $bestlang, it is possible to define a list of languages in order of preference. This list is expressed through the Accept-Language standard[10] [Fielding and Reschke, 2014], in a comma-separated sequence of language codes and weights; for example, en;q=1, it;q=0.7 *;q=0.1 gives a strong preference to English, then to Italian, finally to whatever language is available. Note that in this context en is equivalent to en;q=1, *;q=0.1. $bestlang relies on the non-standard keyword BEST_LANGMATCH, implemented in endpoints like Virtuoso.[11] If $lang may exclude the results without a label in the requested language, $bestlang will return them, proposing an alternative label among the available languages.

For more convenience, the language selection can also be centralized in the root using $lang. This root modifier accepts both a single language code or an Accept-Language string. If present, it becomes the default value for both inline $lang and $bestlang, used in this case without input. This syntax allows to write language-dynamic queries: the root $lang changes according to the selected language without the need to individually change all impacted literal fields, marked once for all with the inline modifiers.

When the language is selected in this way including the language tag in the results may be too verbose by setting the root $langTag modifier as hide, all string literals will be represented as strings, by avoiding the wrapping inside an intermediate object for reporting the language.

5.3.4   A COMPLETE EXAMPLE

Figure 5.5 presents an example of a JSON query that includes several modifiers, in order to see how the different elements interact together. The query retrieves the works present in the Louvre museum—excluding Raphael's ones—together with name, image, and author. For each author, their name and the total number of works are retrieved. It asks for the first 100 results in reverse (descending) alphabetical order of the painting title. This query produces results when used on DBpedia. It is worth noting the following elements.

---

[10]https://tools.ietf.org/html/rfc7231#section-5.3.5
[11]https://virtuoso.openlinksw.com/

```
{                                              PREFIX dbr: <http://dbpedia.org/resource/>
  "proto" : {                                  PREFIX dbo: <http://dbpedia.org/ontology/>
    "id"      : "?work",
    "name"    : "$rdfs:label$required$var:title",   SELECT DISTINCT ?work ?title
    "image"   : "$foaf:depiction$sample",      (SAMPLE(?v2) AS ?v2) ?museum ?author ?v41
    "museum"  : "$dbo:museum$var:museum",       (COUNT(?v42) AS ?v42)
    "author"  : {                              WHERE {
      "uri"   : "$dbo:author$anchor$var:author",     VALUES ?museum {dbr:Louvre}
      "name"  : "$rdfs:label$lang$required",
      "worksCount" : "$dbo:author$reverse$count"     ?work a dbo:Work.
    }                                              ?work rdfs:label ?title.
  },                                             ?work foaf:depiction ?v2.
  "$where"    : "?work a dbo:Work",              ?work dbo:museum ?museum.
  "$filter"   : "?author I= dbr:Raphael",        OPTIONAL {
  "$orderby"  : "desc{?title)",                      ?work dbo:author ?author .
  "$lang"     : "en;q=1, it;q=0.7 *;q=0.1",          ?author rdfs:label ?v41 .
  "$limit"    : 100,                                 FILTER(lang(?v41) = 'en').
  "$values"   : { "museum": "dbr:Louvre" },          ?v42 dbo:author ?author
  "$prefixes" : {                                  }
      "dbr" : "http://dbpedia.org/resource/",
      "dbo" : "http://dbpedia.org/ontology/"       FILTER{?author != dbr:Raphael)
  },                                             }
  "$langTag"  : "hide"                         ORDER BY desc(?title)
}                                              LIMIT 100
```

Figure 5.5: An example of a JSON query (left) with the equivalent SPARQL query (right).

- All variables that need to appear in root modifiers are made explicit with a $var modifier. All the others are automatically assigned by the library (ex. ?v2, ?v41, etc.), so that they cannot be referenced elsewhere in the query.

- $reverse saves adding a triple expression in $where, as we have done in Figure 5.4.

- When not marked with $required, the nodes are transformed into OPTIONAL triples in the SPARQL query. In the case of author.uri (second-level anchor), all triples produced by the nodes in author are wrapped in an optional block.

- We ask for all distinct labels of works, while we want only the English one for the author. The language can be modified for all involved fields from the root $lang.

- The museum is defined in `$values`, acting as a parameter. The value can be easily changed, reusing this query for other museums.

5.4   *grlc* AND *SPARQL TRANSFORMER*

Thanks to the integration between the two technologies, the syntax and the merging mechanism of *SPARQL Transformer* are supported by *grlc*.

A JSON query can be stored in a repository, together with other JSON or SPARQL queries. *grlc* uses the file extension for guessing the query type and applying the proper pipeline. When a JSON query is detected, it is processed by the ST parser. The prototype is stored apart, while the transformed SPARQL query continues to follow the normal *grlc* pipeline. When the results return, they are applied to the stored prototype by the ST shaper, before being served through HTTP.

The selection of API parameters can be done using the `$var` modifier, prepending or appending underscores (`_`) to the variable name, as explained in Section 4.4.2 (example `$var:_museum_iri`). In addition, when a root `$lang` is provided, a `lang` parameter is automatically added to the available ones, making it possible to create multi-language APIs. Other decorators like pagination or description (Section 4.4) can be declared in a separate `"grlc"` attribute at the root level (as a sibling property of `proto`).

As an alternative, it is possible to apply *SPARQL Transformer* shaping and merging to a SPARQL query, by including the desired template in the `transform` decorator. In this way, the standard JSON results will be reshaped to the target format, following the rules described in this chapter. It is particularly important to be sure that an `id` attribute is present or, alternatively, that an `$anchor` is set at each level.

```
#+ summary: Sample query for testing response transformation
#+ endpoint: "http://test-endpoint/transform/sparql/"
#+ transform: {
#+     "key": "?p",
#+     "value": "?o",
#+     "$anchor": "key"
#+ }
select ?p ?o where {
  ?_id_iri ?p ?o
} LIMIT 5
```

5.5   EXERCISES

What follows is a list of exercises for practicing the *SPARQL Transformer* syntax, based on real-world data coming from DBpedia. Take into account that these may be solved in different ways, all of them providing similar results.

For solving the exercises, it is possible to use the **SPARQL Transformer Playground**,[12] a web application for writing and testing JSON queries. The application provides live conversion into SPARQL while writing, the possibility to retrieve results, and a comparison between the original and reshaped data. All solutions are in Appendix A.

Exercise 5.1 Write a JSON query equivalent to the following SPARQL query.

```
SELECT DISTINCT *
WHERE {
    ?id a dbo:Band.
    ?id rdfs:label ?band_label.
    ?id dbo:genre ?genre .
    ?genre rdfs:label ?genre_label
}
LIMIT 100
```

Exercise 5.2 For each NBA player, retrieve his URI identifier, name, a single image (if available) and his birth date (if available).
Tip: you may want to start by looking at LeBron James in DBpedia.

Exercise 5.3 For each team in the NBA,[13] retrieve the name of the team and the the id and name for all players of the team. For any name, be sure to pick the best label for an English-speaking public. Improve the readability of results by hiding the language tag.

Exercise 5.4 For each country using the Euro as currency,[14] retrieve its id, name, and the list of its cities, together with city names and populations. Make sure to pick exactly the English labels and to hide the language tag. Limit the results to the first 100.
Tip: you may start by looking at Athens in DBpedia.

Exercise 5.5 For each country using the Euro as currency, retrieve the id, the name, and the total number of cities in the country. Order by descending number of cities. Make sure to pick exactly the English labels and to hide the language tag.

Exercise 5.6 Retrieve the list of Italian regions, their names and the list of cities in the region (id + label). Limit to the first 100 results and pick labels in Italian, hiding the language tag. Use the JSON-LD syntax. Make sure that your query is easily extensible to other countries and languages, for example France and French or United States and English.
Tip: you may start by looking at Piedmont in DBpedia.

---

[12] https://d2klab.github.io/sparql-transformer/
[13] ?team dct:subject dbc:National_Basketball_Association_teams
[14] ?country dbo:currency dbr:Euro

CHAPTER 6

Applications

The tools and principles that we have explained in this book, in particular those that facilitated the creation of the tools *grlc* (described in Chapter 4) and *SPARQL Transformer* (described in Chapter 5), originated in research programs around Knowledge Graphs and the Semantic Web, in particular the Dutch national program CLARIAH[1] [Meroño-Peñuela et al., 2020] and the French project DOREMUS (DOing REusable MUSical data)[2] [Achichi et al., 2018], from 2016 onward.

Ever since, we have observed adoption of these methods and tools, often beyond the limits of their incubating projects in a number of application domains in various projects, companies, and institutions. For example, from the start of its operation in July 2016, the public instance of *grlc*[3] has attracted 4,948 unique visitors, 39.92% of return rate, and generating 9,840 sessions. *grlc* has also attracted the attention of external developers, who have sent 147 pull requests that have been integrated into the master branch. Its docker container has been pulled 2.5K times.[4] A list of community maintained queries and matching APIs is available at https://git.io/grlc-usage, currently counting 444 publicly shared queries. *SPARQL Transformer* has been downloaded from npm and *PyPI* thousands of times since 2017 (an average of 100 downloads per month).

In this chapter, we describe some of the most relevant success cases in the application of the methods and tools described in this book, extending on previously published cases [Lisena et al., 2019, Meroño-Peñuela and Hoekstra, 2017]. For each of these cases, we explain what the challenges are and what the situation was before and after deploying solution based on these methods and tools, emphasizing the specific requirements that were considered critical and the extent to which they were addressed. We group them in three categories: applications of *grlc*; applications of *SPARQL Transformer*; and applications that leverage the combined capabilities of both. We end the chapter with a reference table with links to relevant sources of code, documentation, tools, and examples.

---

[1] https://clariah.nl
[2] https://www.doremus.org
[3] https://grlc.io
[4] https://hub.docker.com/r/clariah/grlc

6.1   *grlc*

6.1.1   LINKED DATA PLATFORM FOR GENETICS RESEARCH

In genetics research, it is increasingly common to analyze fully sequenced genomes and identify traits associated with specific genes. However, information about genetic traits is usually available in disparate sources, such as scientific literature and in public biological databases. Genomics researchers need to combine these information sources in order to identify genes of particular interest.

Researchers from the Plant Breeding group at Wageningen University and the Netherlands eScience Center built a Linked Data platform called *pbg-ld* which combines data extracted from Europe PubMed Central (PMC) repository and genomic annotations from the Sol Genomics Network (SGN), UniProt, and Ensembl Plants databases. This analytical platform allowed its users to access relevant information on *Solanaceae* species.

A collection of SPARQL queries[5] powers this platform, allowing users to count genomic features in a genome graph, extract the genomic location of specific features, and extract annotations from specific genes, among other features. Users do not need to understand or modify the SPARQL queries, but instead are able to access the data directly through a web API. A Jupyter notebook queries the API endpoints, and presents results to the users in the form of summary tables or bar charts.

This platform provides users with a way to access the most used datasets for candidate gene discovery in tomato and potato species. In turn, this increases the transparency for users who wish to visualize data on this platform or extend this tool for other crop species.

Further details of this example can be found in Singh et al. [2020].

6.1.2   NANOPUBLICATIONS

Nanopublications [Groth et al., 2010] are a Linked Data format for scholarly data publishing that has received considerable uptake in the last few years. In contrast to common Linked Data publishing practice, nanopublications consist of atomic information snippets of assertion data, providing a container format to link provenance information and metadata to those assertions. While the nanopublications format is domain-independent, the datasets that have become available in this format are mostly from Life Science domains, including data about diseases, genes, proteins, drugs, biological pathways, and biotic interactions. More than 10 million such nanopublications have been published, which now form a valuable resource for studies on the domain level of the given Life Science domains as well as on the more technical levels of provenance modeling and heterogeneous Linked Data.

In order to facilitate easier and more powerful access to nanopublications, Kuhn et al. [2018] provided a Linked Data API to access the full set of nanopublications available on the network. This API is powered by a *grlc* server in front of a GraphDB triple store instance with a SPARQL endpoint.[6] This API offers a standard entry point to the data in the nanopublications network, which any Linked

---

[5]https://github.com/candYgene/queries
[6]The API is available at http://purl.org/nanopub/api; the underlying parametrized queries can be found at https://github.com/peta-pico/nanopub-api/.

```
46  ## using grlc API call
47  library(RCurl)
48  canada <- getURL("http://grlc.clariah-sdh.eculture.labs.vu.nl/chariah/wpr-
49  canada <- read.csv(textConnection(canada))
50  sweden <- getURL("http://grlc.clariah-sdh.eculture.labs.vu.nl/chariah/wpr-
51  sweden <- read.csv(textConnection(sweden))
52
53  fit_canada_base <- lm(log(hiscam) ~ log(gdppc), data=canada)
54  fit_canada <- lm(log(hiscam) ~ log(gdppc) + I(age^2) + age, data=canada)
55  fit_sweden_base <- lm(log(hiscam) ~ log(gdppc), data=sweden)
56  fit_sweden <- lm(log(hiscam) ~ log(gdppc) + I(age^2) + age, data=sweden)
```

Figure 6.1: The use of *grlc* makes Knowledge Graphs accessible from any `http` compatible application.

Data client can consume via HTTP without specific knowledge of SPARQL or RDF. A Python package[7] integrates publishing and retracting nanopublications from the network using *grlc*, together with many other features.

6.1.3   CLARIAH AND SOCIAL HISTORY RESEARCH

The International Institute for Social History partners in the CLARIAH[8] project for building a large national infrastructure for data in the arts and the digital humanities. CLARIAH has been essential in the development of *grlc*, in terms of funding and resources, and also by providing its first use cases.

Typical social history research requires querying across combined, structured humanities data, and performing statistical analysis in, e.g., R [Hoekstra et al., 2016, 2018]. A typical social history use cases focuses on validating the hypothesis that prenatal and early-life conditions have a strong impact on socio economic and health outcomes later in life, by using 1891 census records of Canada and Sweden. Given that there are potentially infinitely many such research queries, building a one-size-fits-all API is not feasible. Before *grlc*, this required manual downloading of SPARQL result data to a CSV file, for post-hoc analysis in R. The R SPARQL package [van Hage et al., 2013] allows one to use SPARQL queries directly from R. However, this results in hard-coded, non reusable, and difficult to maintain queries. After better organizing these queries in a GitHub repository, an API using them became immediately available through *grlc*. As shown in Figure 6.1, with *grlc* the R code becomes clearer due to the decoupling with SPARQL; and shorter, since a `curl` one-liner calling a *grlc* enabled API operation suffices to retrieve the data. Furthermore, the exact query feeding the research results can be stored and shared with fellow scholars and in papers.

---

[7]https://github.com/fair-workflows/nanopub
[8]http://clariah.nl/

6.1.4   TNO: FOODCUBE

The Netherlands Organisation for Applied Scientific Research (TNO) uses *grlc* in a project about food for the municipality of Almere [Wapenaar, 2017]. FoodCube aims to provide an integrated view to all kinds of datasets related to the food supply chain—domain knowledge and interesting domain questions are the core focus. FoodCube uses *grlc* to provide "FAQ" (Frequently Asked SPARQL Questions) for those who would prefer REST over SPARQL, but also to explore the data. This is made possible by the ability to annotate the SPARQL queries with keywords and a description.

6.1.5   NEWGEN CHENNAI: CONFERENCE PROCEEDINGS

NewGen[9] uses *grlc* to build the IOS Press ECAI API. Their goal is to expose the ECAI conference proceedings not only as Linked Data that can be used by Semantic Web practitioners, but also as a Web API that general Web developers can consume. This is useful for bringing together both communities, and making their rich software ecosystems mutually compatible. Key features of *grlc* for this use case are query curation, sharing and dissemination. For this last point, being able to provide metadata to individual queries is reportedly very useful. NewGen finds it easy to set-up, document, and use the API. Similarly, the use of git as a backend is an advantage, and they consider the *grlc* development community helpful. Other plausible alternatives were considered,[10] but the two advantages of *grlc* were its use of GitHub for re-using queries curated by the community, and the minimum infrastructure/resources needed for automatically building APIs from them.

6.1.6   EU RISIS: SCIENCE, TECHNOLOGY, AND INNOVATION

grlc was used as a component of the Semantically Mapping Science (SMS) platform[11] for sharing of SPARQL queries and thereby their results among multiple researchers. At the technical core of the RISIS EU project [van den Besselaar and Khalili, 2018],[12] SMS provides a data integration platform where researchers from science, technology, and innovation (STI) can find answers to their research questions. This platform provides a faceted data browser where interactions of non-linked data-expert users are translated into a set of complex SPARQL queries, which are then run to aggregate data from relevant SPARQL endpoints [Khalili and Meroño-Peñuela, 2017]. One of the challenges within the platform was how to share, extend and repurpose user-generated queries in a flexible way. *grlc* addresses this challenge by providing a URI as a reference and encapsulation unit for each individual query, and by supporting a collaborative editing of the contents of those queries.

---

[9]https://www.newgen.co
[10]Reportedly https://github.com/danistrebel/SemanticGraphQL, https://github.com/nelson-ai/semantic-graphql, and https://github.com/ColinMaudry/sparql-router/wiki/Using-SPARQL-router.
[11]http://sms.risis.eu
[12]http://risis.eu

6.2   SPARQL TRANSFORMER

6.2.1   KG EXPLORER

KG Explorer[13] is a web-based exploratory search engine for Knowledge Graphs, entirely realized using web technologies (JavaScript, HTML, and CSS). The application stands in front of a SPARQL Endpoint and offers to the final user the possibility to explore the dataset through a user interface. Available features are a facet-based advanced search, a dedicated page for controlled vocabularies in SKOS, a customized detail page, the possibility to create lists of favorites.

The software can be configured in order to adapt to different information domains, as happened with ADASilk[14] for data about silk heritage and MeMAD Explorer[15] for data about TV programs. The configuration of KG Explorer involves different parts of the application, from the available languages to the color theme, to eventual plugins to be loaded. Even the queries used in the application can be adapted, in order to have detail pages reporting all relevant information—beyond direct property links—and better implementing the available filters for the advanced search. Given that this configuration is based on a single JavaScript file, *SPARQL Transformer* was the more obvious choice for expressing those queries.

For the sake of example, Listing 6.1 contains an extract of a configuration file,[16] in particular the definition of the search view from entity with type `ecrm:E22_Man-Made_Object`. A base query is defined for retrieving the first set of results, with label, identifier, description, etc. When a filter is applied, this query is modified applying new `WHERE` and `FILTER` expressions, respectively defined in `whereFunc` and `filterFunc`. The use of JSON queries makes it possible to simply append this expression to the `$where` and `$filter` properties, and avoids a much more complex manipulation of text which the use of plain SPARQL queries would require.

In addition to this, the application development largely benefit from the merging capabilities of *SPARQL Transformer*, having to deal with a more handy object.

6.2.2   FADE

FADE (Filling Automatically Dialog Events)[17] is a component for chatbot applications for extracting data from a Knowledge Graph. Its core feature consists of the automatic extraction of dictionaries of entries which are then processed by the natural language unit (NLU). FADE is integrated in the tourist assistant MinoTour.[18]

A configuration file in JSON is used to define the different *intents*.[19] The terms that refer to entities and that need to be recognized by the NLU are extracted with *SPARQL Transformer*. The

---

[13]https://github.com/D2KLab/explorer

[14]https://git.io/adasilk

[15]https://git.io/memad-explorer

[16]The code is extracted from the ADASilk configuration and is fully available at https://github.com/silknow/adasilk/blob/main/config/routes/object.js.

[17]https://github.com/ehrhart/fade

[18]https://minotour.eurecom.fr/

[19]In chatbot development, an *intent* is the goal that the user wants to achieve when sending a message to the system. An important part of chatbot development is indeed the *intent detection*, which aims to assign to each message the right goal.

```
{
    view: 'browse', // 'browse' creates a search page
    showInNavbar: true,
    rdfType: 'ecrm:E22_Man-Made_Object',
    uriBase: 'http://data.silknow.org/object',
    filters: [{  // filters to appear in the advanced search
      id: 'material',
      whereFunc: () => [ // added to the base query
        '?production ecrm:P126_employed ?material',
        'OPTIONAL { ?broaderMaterial (skos:member|skos:narrower)*
            ?material }'
      ],
      filterFunc: (values) => { // added to the base query
        return [values.map((val) =>
        `?material = <${val}> || ?broaderMaterial = <${val}>`).
          join(' || ')];
    }}],
    query: { // base query
        '@graph': [{
            '@type': 'ecrm:E22_Man-Made_Object',
            '@id': '?id',
            '@graph': '?g',
            label: '$rdfs:label',
            identifier: '$dc:identifier',
            description: '$ecrm:P3_has_note',
        }],
        $where: 'GRAPH ?g { ?id a ecrm:E22_Man-Made_Object }'
    }
}
```

Listing 6.1: Extract of the ADASilk configuration showing the usage of *SPARQL Transformer* in KG Explorer.

JSON query is directly included in the JSON configuration and the output values are shaped in order to fit the data structure expected by the other components. The merging capabilities are crucial for correctly handling synonyms for the same entity.

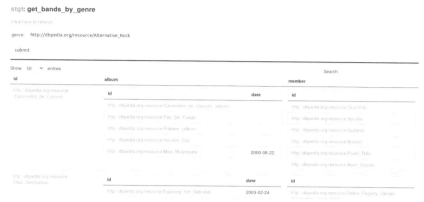

Figure 6.2: **Screenshot of the Tapas interface** (from Lisena et al. [2019]).

6.3   *grlc* AND *TRANSFORMER*

The most significant application of the integrated capabilities of *grlc* and *SPARQL Transformer* is Tapas, a Web interface for quick and customized API interfaces.[20] Tapas (shown in Figure 6.2) is an HTML and JavaScript module capable of reading OpenAPI specifications from *grlc* APIs, turning them into nice and simple HTML interfaces. The elements of the API specification are straightforwardly transformed into HTML form elements, which the user can fill in to access the service by pressing the *submit* button. Tapas asynchronously calls the API via *grlc* and shows the results at the bottom part of the same page using the YASR component of the YASGUI interface [Rietveld and Hoekstra, 2017] to display the SPARQL query results in a user-friendly manner. The results are rendered according to the *SPARQL Transformer* specifications. In the experiments reported in Lisena et al. [2019], the authors show that users with a mixed SPARQL and JSON background prefer these kinds of interfaces that return and show query results with some degree of object nesting, according to their needs.

6.4   DEMOS/LINKS

Table 6.1 includes all links referring to resources and tools presented in this book. Of particular relevance to the reader who wants to solidify the concepts already seen in this book, we point out the Tutorial *SPARQL Endpoints and Web APIs (SWApi)*, which took place at the *19th International Semantic Web Conference (ISWC 2020)*. The website offers teaching material and also video tutorials about *SPARQL Transformer* and *grlc*.

---

[20]https://github.com/peta-pico/tapas

Table 6.1: Links to resources and tools presented in this book

Name	URL
grlc	
grlc website	`https://grlc.io/`
Demo api	`https://grlc.io/api-git/CLARIAH/grlc-queries/`
Repository	`https://github.com/CLARIAH/grlc`
grlc queries in GitHub	`https://git.io/grlc-usage`
Docker Image	`https://hub.docker.com/r/clariah/grlc`
SPARQL Transformer	
Repository (JS)	`https://github.com/D2KLab/sparql-transformer`
Repository (Python)	`https://github.com/D2KLab/py-sparql-transformer`
Playground	`https://d2klab.github.io/sparql-transformer`
SWApi Tutorial	`https://api4kg.github.io/swapi-tutorial/` (with videos)
Example and Exercises	`https://github.com/api4kg/exercises`

CHAPTER 7

Conclusion and Future Challenges

What have we learned in this book?

In Chapter 1, we briefly presented Knowledge Graphs as a paradigm for publishing structured and semantically rich data on the Web, and query languages (in particular SPARQL) as a means to access the wealth of information in those Knowledge Graphs. We also pointed out some of the challenges that developers face when using these query languages, and in particular how they differ with the overwhelmingly common paradigm of Web Data APIs.

In Chapter 2, we dived deeper into how developers interact with SPARQL and Knowledge Graphs in a programmatic fashion. We reviewed how to use HTTP requests to send SPARQL queries to Knowledge Graph endpoints, and how to process HTTP responses to consume their returned data in JSON format. Since preparing these SPARQL HTTP requests and processing their JSON responses can be quite tedious, we surveyed libraries in different programming languages that help developers in dealing with them. These libraries became, then, a first layer of abstraction in managing Knowledge Graph queries and responses.

In Chapter 3, we saw, however, that these libraries are often not enough to bridge the wide gap between SPARQL and REST APIs. To understand why this is the case, we described the OpenAPI specification—the *de facto* standard for REST APIs—and we manually built a REST API on top of SPARQL, adding yet another abstraction layer in query management. However, this came with the price of repetitive labor, lack of query management and documentation (e.g., the need of maintaining a proper mapping between SPARQL template variables and OpenAPI parameters), and the inability to control the data structures of JSON results.

In Chapter 4, we looked at ways of addressing the first two challenges: avoid repetitive labor when building APIs on top of SPARQL; and managing queries, their documentation, and their mapping to the OpenAPI standard. To this end we presented *grlc*, a lightweight server that automatically builds Web Data APIs by leveraging SPARQL queries that are published on the Web and that explicitly document their mapping with OpenAPI features. This method can be used for both building API specifications and executing API calls, and adds yet another layer of query management and processing that developers need not worry about.

In Chapter 5, we dealt with the last challenge: how to control the shape of the data structures returned by SPARQL queries as JSON results. To this end, we introduced *SPARQL Transformer*, an approach that declaratively maps the body of SPARQL queries and their desired JSON output within one unique JSON object. This allows an arbitrary restructuring of JSON objects in a way that is transparent to SPARQL endpoints, adding another layer that can work in conjunction with *grlc* and query management.

In Chapter 6, we reviewed a number of applications of these tools in real-world applications and use cases, providing links to abundant documentation, code, and resources. The chapter shows that there is a large developer community that is very keen on using Knowledge Graphs through APIs, provided adequate tooling is in place to make this easier for them.

But beyond this chapter breakdown, let us recall the important question we posed in Chapter 1: **Can *any* developer query Knowledge Graphs?** A proper survey is probably needed to give a fair answer to this question, but we may take the current wide gap—in practices and knowledge—between general Web API developers and SPARQL developers as proof that, indeed, *not* any developer can today query Knowledge Graphs—at least, not easily enough. The practices and knowledge of these two communities are very much related, but differ in practice too often in ways that are hard to reconcile. Some discussions about this gap have emphasized the differences between the two communities—e.g., the expressivity of REST vs. SPARQL, client-server load balancing, federation—these discussions are good from an intellectual point of view, because they help us to better understand requirements and opportunities for research. The current momentum and flourishing of graph query languages (SPARQL, but also GraphQL, Cypher, Gremlin, and a long etc.) can only make us think that learning these, and the ones to come, can only do good to the current ecosystem of Knowledge Graphs and graph databases. However, the discussion between these two communities often turns confrontational instead of focusing on the *commonalities* between the two communities: a shared vision of Web structured knowledge, available for querying to any developer that wishes to use it to bring intelligent applications to a next level. The paradigm shift from a Web of text to a Web of knowledge is still a common goal through many developers; but we may need small, cumulative, harmonizing and convergent steps towards it, rather than radical and disruptive solutions.[1] This very much overlaps with the reasoning and ideas behind the Easier RDF initiative[2] [Booth et al., 2019] of the W3C. This is, in our view, the way to make the community of Knowledge Graph developers grow, which in turn benefits the maturity of the infrastructure to access Knowledge Graphs, bringing in more applications, users, and success stories.

With this book, it was our purpose to explain the tools, principles, and abstraction layers that we have contributed in recent years and have found useful to bridge that gap. We sincerely hope that both communities—Web API and SPARQL developers—find it useful to continue bringing both worlds closer together.

In light of all we have seen, we can only be optimistic about the future of Web Data APIs for accessing Knowledge Graphs in terms of new graph representations and query paradigms and languages; and new principles and engineering components to add to the SPARQL-API bridging pipeline that we have presented in this book. Some directions that we foresee include the progress of varied Knowledge Graph querying infrastructures; query management for Knowledge Graphs; and the specification of standard SPARQL-API mapping languages.

---

[1]This is particularly true in, e.g., Apache Neptune [Bebee et al., 2018], which explicitly embraces diversity and sets the path toward unifying RDF, RDF-star and Property Graphs and, consequently, Gremlin and SPARQL.

[2]https://github.com/w3c/EasierRDF

It is clear that a growing ecosystem of query languages and paradigms and varying degrees of developer expertise in them calls for **Knowledge Graph querying infrastructures that value and leverage heterogeneity of access methods**. For example, in Chapter 4 we saw that the availability of SPARQL and REST API interfaces does not necessarily need to come at the expense of each other: both can co-exist within a Knowledge Graph querying ecosystem and leverage their inter-dependence for better maintainability. We achieved this by adding layers of abstraction and separation of concerns to currently existing interfaces—all well-known software engineering principles. Their continued application can foster Knowledge Graphs with more varied and better maintained access interfaces in a number of different scenarios. For example, novel architectures like RAMOSE [Daquino et al., 2020] emphasize the need for query result *post-processing* in the interface pipeline. From a different angle, the Easier RDF community gathers ideas around the fact that RDF and SPARQL continue to be niche technologies (as we pointed out in Chapter 2) that need to be easier to use for average developers [Booth et al., 2019].

Consequently, many ideas that we have presented in this book point toward the need for establishing a systematic and principled **Knowledge Graph query management process** in its own right. As we progressed from Chapter 2 to Chapter 5, it became more and more clear that Knowledge Graph APIs can be better built and maintained if queries are externally managed by dedicated systems; and if they are richly and structurally documented (by, e.g., adding metadata about what they do, what parameters they accept, what default endpoint they were written for, how their responses should be represented in JSON, etc.). Thinking about good principles of data management, one can only consider a wider, more encompassing curation of queries: keeping good track of their versioning and provenance; of their associated permissions and public/private access; of their equivalence relationship with implementations in other languages (e.g., this query is available in SPARQL, Gremlin, GraphQL, etc.); and so on. Moreover, the open setting of the Web and the inherent public character of most (though not all) Knowledge Graphs suggest that this query management might be better dealt with in a distributed fashion, instead than in a central, unique repository. In our case, this led us to use the well-known principle of indirection. In Chapter 4, we used URIs as unique global identifiers to *represent* a SPARQL query and its associated metadata on the Web; in this way, remote systems can reliably retrieve (using HTTP) the contents of the query in a stable manner, even if these contents change over time. Indeed, publishing and versioning queries provided many advantages in terms of transparency and reproducible research. First of all, it provided separation of concerns: with the queries being published online and separate from the application logic, any application which makes use of the data can be decoupled from SPARQL syntax and use the data by simply calling a URL. Online publishing through dedicated query management systems also provided transparency, which is of fundamental importance for Open Science: any person interested in where the data is coming from and how it is being processed can have access to the query, inspect it and understand what is happening under the hood. Finally, keeping queries under version control helped support reproducible research: it allowed researchers to identify the exact version of the query which was used to produce a specific result. Researchers interested in reproducing these results at a later stage are now able to find the exact version of the query originally used, and can use it to reproduce the results in question.

Many of the ideas presented in this book point toward **the need for more pragmatic and explicit SPARQL-API mapping standard languages**, and possibly toward the need for other mapping standard languages. As we added more and more features to *grlc* and *SPARQL Transformer*, we saw that, in practice, we were just translating different features of the OpenAPI specification (e.g., parameters, response schemas) as metadata decorators for SPARQL queries. Here it is highly relevant to mention the work of the W3C Declarative Linked Data apps community group, pushing for Linked Data standards in this direction [Jusevičius, 2020], and Linked Data Reactor [Khalili and de Graaf, 2017] for declarative UI specifications. Obviously, these mappings might be needed not just for SPARQL and the OpenAPI specification: for example, other experiences show that this can also be done between OWL (which is uniquely equipped to define entity types with `owl:Class`) and REST APIs [Espinoza-Arias et al., 2020]. We think that declarative languages that help in mapping these feature equivalences between different querying paradigms can contribute to the aforementioned ecosystem of interdependent, heterogeneous, and highly maintainable Knowledge Graph access interfaces.

APPENDIX A

Solutions

A.1 CHAPTER 4

Exercise 4.1 Create an API that retrieves all bands from DBpedia.
Tip: Use the DBpedia ontology type `dbo:Band`.

Solution 4.1

```
#+ summary: Lists all DBpedia dbo:Band
#+ endpoint: http://dbpedia.org/sparql
#+ method: GET

PREFIX dbo: <http://dbpedia.org/ontology/>

SELECT DISTINCT ?s
WHERE {
  ?s a dbo:Band
}
```

Exercise 4.2 Create an API that lists bands that play either Rock or Jazz, and that have either Liverpool or Los Angeles as hometown.
Tip 1: Use the DBpedia ontology types `dbo:genre` and `dbo:hometown`.
Tip 2: Use the *grlc* `enumerate` decorator.

Solution 4.2

```
#+ summary: Bands by city and genre
#+ endpoint: http://dbpedia.org/sparql
#+ tags:
#+   - dbpedia
#+ method: GET
#+ enumerate:
#+   - genre:
#+       - http://dbpedia.org/resource/Rock_music
#+       - http://dbpedia.org/resource/Jazz
#+   - hometown:
```

```
#+        - http://dbpedia.org/resource/Liverpool
#+        - http://dbpedia.org/resource/Los_Angeles

PREFIX dbo: <http://dbpedia.org/ontology/>
SELECT DISTINCT ?s
WHERE {
  ?s a dbo:Band;
  dbo:genre ?_genre_iri;
  dbo:hometown ?_hometown_iri
}
```

Exercise 4.3 Expand the API from the previous exercise by adding documentation and making sure your query can only be run on DBpedia SPARQL endpoint.

Tip: Use the summary, description, endpoint, and endpoint_in_url decorators.

Solution 4.3

```
#+ summary: Bands by city and genre
#+ description:
#+   This API endpoint lists bands from DBPedia
#+   that play either Rock or Jazz, and that have
#+   either Liverpool or Los Angeles as hometown.
#+ endpoint: http://dbpedia.org/sparql
#+ endpoint_in_url: false
#+ tags:
#+   - dbpedia
#+ method: GET
#+ enumerate:
#+   - genre:
#+      - http://dbpedia.org/resource/Rock_music
#+      - http://dbpedia.org/resource/Jazz
#+   - hometown:
#+      - http://dbpedia.org/resource/Liverpool
#+      - http://dbpedia.org/resource/Los_Angeles

PREFIX dbo: <http://dbpedia.org/ontology/>
SELECT DISTINCT ?s
WHERE {
  ?s a dbo:Band;
  dbo:genre ?_genre_iri;
```

```
        dbo:hometown ?_hometown_iri
}
```

Exercise 4.4 Create an API that lists the name, genre and hometown of bands whose name matches a given string.

Tip 1: Use the DBpedia property type *dbp:name*.

Tip 2: Because DBpedia uses Virtuoso, you can use the built in function *bif:contains*[1]

Solution 4.4

```
#+  summary: Bands by city and genre
#+  description:
#+    This API endpoint lists bands from DBPedia
#+    that play either Rock or Jazz, and that have
#+    either Liverpool or Los Angeles as hometown.
#+  endpoint: http://dbpedia.org/sparql
#+  endpoint_in_url: false
#+  tags:
#+    - dbpedia
#+  method: GET


PREFIX dbo: <http://dbpedia.org/ontology/>
PREFIX dbp: <http://dbpedia.org/property/>
PREFIX bif: <bif:>

SELECT DISTINCT ?name ?genre ?hometown
WHERE {
?s a dbo:Band;
  dbp:name ?name;
  dbo:genre ?genre;
  dbo:hometown ?hometown .
  ?name bif:contains ?_bandname
} LIMIT 100
```

A.2   CHAPTER 5

Exercise 5.1 Write a JSON query equivalent to the following SPARQL query.

[1]http://docs.openlinksw.com/virtuoso/rdfsparqlrulefulltext/

```
SELECT DISTINCT *
WHERE {
    ?id a dbo:Band.
    ?id rdfs:label ?band_label.
    ?id dbo:genre ?genre .
    ?genre rdfs:label ?genre_label
}
LIMIT 100
```

Solution 5.1

```
{
  "proto": {
    "id": "?id",
    "label": "$rdfs:label$required",
    "genre": {
        "id": "$dbo:genre$required",
        "label": "$rdfs:label$required"
    }
  },
  "$where": "?id a dbo:Band",
  "$limit": 100
}
```

Exercise 5.2 For each NBA player, retrieve his URI identifier, name, a single image (if available), and his birth date (if available).

Tip: you may want to start by looking at LeBron James in DBpedia.

Solution 5.2

```
{
  "proto": {
    "id": "?id",
    "name": "$rdfs:label$required",
    "league": "$dbo:league$var:league",
    "image": "$foaf:depiction$sample",
    "birthDate": "$dbo:birthDate"
  },
  "$values": {
    "league":"dbr:National_Basketball_Association"
```

```
   }
 }
```

Exercise 5.3 For each team in NBA, retrieve the name of the team and the id and name for all players of the team. For any name, be sure to pick the best label for an English-speaking public. Improve results readability by hiding the language tag.

Solution 5.3

```
{
   "proto": {
      "team" : "?team$anchor",
      "name": "$rdfs:label$required$bestlang",
      "players" : {
        "id": "$dbo:team$reverse",
        "name": "$rdfs:label$required$bestlang"
      }
   },
   "$where": "?team dct:subject dbc:
      National_Basketball_Association_teams",
   "$lang": "en",
   "$langTag": "hide"
}
```

Exercise 5.4 For each country using the Euro as currency,[2] retrieve its id, name, and list of its cities, together with city names and populations. Make sure to pick exactly the English labels and to hide the language tag. Limit the results to the first 100.

Tip: you may start by looking at Athens in DBpedia.

Solution 5.4

```
{
   "proto": {
     "state": "?state$anchor",
     "name": "$rdfs:label$required$lang:en",
     "cities": {
         "id": "$dbo:country$reverse$var:city$required",
         "name": "$rdfs:label$required$lang:en",
         "population": "$dbo:populationTotal$required" }
```

---

[2] ?country dbo:currency dbr:Euro

```
    },
    "$where": [
            "?state dbo:currency dbr:Euro",
            "?city a  dbo:City" ] ,
    "$langTag": "hide",
    "$limit" : 100
}
```

Exercise 5.5 For each country using the Euro as currency, retrieve the id, the name, and the total number of cities in the country. Order by descending number of cities. Make sure to pick exactly the English labels and to hide the language tag.

Solution 5.5

```
{
  "proto": {
    "state": "?state$anchor",
    "name": "$rdfs:label$required$lang:en",
    "cities":   "$dbo:country$reverse$var:city$count"
  },
  "$where": [
      "?state dbo:currency dbr:Euro",
      "?city a dbo:City"
  ] ,
  "$orderby" : "desc(?city)",
  "$langTag": "hide"
}
```

Exercise 5.6 Retrieve the list of Italian regions, with names and the list of cities in the region (id + label). Limit to the first 100 results and pick labels in Italian, hiding the language tag. Use the JSON-LD syntax. Make sure that your query is easily extensible to other countries and languages, for example France and French or United States and English.
Tip: you may start by looking at Piedmont in DBpedia.

Solution 5.6

```
{
  "@context": "http://example.org/",
  "@graph": [{
   "@type": "AdministrativeArea",
   "@id": "?id",
   "name": "$rdfs:label$required$lang",
   "country":"$dbo:country$required$var:country",
   "city": {
    "@id":"$dbo:region$required$reverse$var:city",
    "name": "$rdfs:label$required$lang"
    }
  }],
  "$where": [
    "?id a dbo:AdministrativeRegion",
    "?city a dbo:City"
  ],
  "$values" : {
    "country" : "dbr:Italy"
  },
  "$lang": "it",
  "$langTag": "hide",
  "$limit": 100
}
```

Bibliography

Manel Achichi, Pasquale Lisena, Konstantin Todorov, Raphaël Troncy, and Jean Delahousse. DORE-MUS: A graph of linked musical works. In *17th International Semantic Web Conference (ISWC)*, Monterey, CA, October 2018. DOI: 10.1007/978-3-030-00668-6_1 65

Stanislav Barton. Indexing structure for discovering relationships in RDF graph recursively applying tree transformation. In *Semantic Web Workshop at 27th Annual International ACM SIGIR Conference*, pages 58–68, Desna, Czech Republic, 2004. 49

Bradley R. Bebee, Daniel Choi, Ankit Gupta, Andi Gutmans, Ankesh Khandelwal, Yigit Kiran, Sainath Mallidi, Bruce McGaughy, Mike Personick, Karthik Rajan, et al. Amazon neptune: Graph data management in the cloud. In *17th International Semantic Web Conference (ISWC), P&D/Industry/BlueSky*, 2018. 74

David Beckett. RDF 1.1 N-triples. W3C Recommendation, World Wide Web Consortium, 2014. https://www.w3.org/TR/n-triples 3, 4, 6, 14

GO Blog. Introducing the knowledge graph: Things, not strings, 2012. https://blog.google/products/search/introducing-knowledge-graph-things-not/ 2

David Booth, Christopher G. Chute, Hugh Glaser, and Harold Solbrig. Toward easier RDF. In *W3C Workshop on Web Standardization for Graph Data*, Berlin, Germany, 2019. xv, 74, 75

Pierre Bourhis, Juan L. Reutter, Fernando Suárez, and Domagoj Vrgoč. JSON: data model, query languages and schema specification. In *36th ACM SIGMOD-SIGACT-SIGAI Symposium on Principles of Database Systems*, pages 123–135, 2017. DOI: 10.1145/3034786.3056120 xv

Dan Brickley and R. V. Guha. RDF schema 1.1. *W3C Recommendation*, World Wide Web Consortium, 2014. https://www.w3.org/TR/rdf-schema/ 3

Jeen Broekstra, Arjohn Kampman, and Frank van Harmelen. Sesame: A generic architecture for storing and querying RDF and RDF schema. In Ian Horrocks and James Hendler, Eds., *1st International Semantic Web Conference (ISWC)*, pages 54–68, Springer Berlin Heidelberg, 2002. DOI: 10.1007/3-540-48005-6_7 49

Gavin Carothers. RDF 1.1 N-Quads. A line-based syntax for RDF datasets. *W3C Recommendation*, World Wide Web Consortium, 2014. http://www.w3.org/TR/2014/REC-n-quads-20140225/

Richard Cyganiak, David Wood, and Markus Lanthaler. RDF 1.1 Concepts and Abstract Syntax. Technical report, World Wide Web Consortium (W3C), 2014. http://www.w3.org/TR/rdf11-concepts/ xv

Marilena Daquino, Ivan Heibi, Silvio Peroni, and David Shotton. Creating RESTful APIs over SPARQL endpoints with RAMOSE. *ArXiv Preprint ArXiv:2007.16079*, 2020. 75

Bob DuCharme. *Learning SPARQL: Querying and Updating with SPARQL 1.1.* O'Reilly Media, Inc., 2013. 7

Paola Espinoza-Arias, Daniel Garijo, and Oscar Corcho. Mapping the web ontology language to the OpenAPI specification. In *International Conference on Conceptual Modeling*, pages 117–127, Springer, 2020. DOI: 10.1007/978-3-030-65847-2_11 76

Javier D. Fernández, Wouter Beek, Miguel A. Martínez-Prieto, and Mario Arias. LOD-a-lot: A queryable dump of the LOD cloud. In *16th International Semantic Web Conference (ISWC)*, pages 75–83, Springer, 2017. DOI: 10.1007/978-3-319-68204-4_7 xvii, 2

Roy Fielding and Julian Reschke. Hypertext transfer protocol (HTTP/1.1): Semantics and content. RFC 7231, RFC Editor, June 2014. https://tools.ietf.org/html/rfc7231 61

Roy T. Fielding and Richard N. Taylor. *Architectural Styles and the Design of Network-Based Software Architectures*, volume 7. University of California, Irvine, 2000. 25

Paul Groth, Andrew Gibson, and Jan Velterop. The anatomy of a nanopublication. *Information Services and Use*, 30(1–2):51–56, 2010. DOI: 10.3233/isu-2010-0613 66

Ramanathan V. Guha, Dan Brickley, and Steve Macbeth. Schema.org: Evolution of structured data on the Web. *Communications of the ACM*, 59(2):44–51, 2016. DOI: 10.1145/2844544 2

Claudio Gutierrez and Juan F. Sequeda. Knowledge graphs: A tutorial on the history of knowledge graph's main ideas. In *29th ACM International Conference on Information and Knowledge Management (CIKM)*, pages 3509–3510, 2020. DOI: 10.1145/3340531.3412176 1, 2

Florian Haupt, Frank Leymann, and Cesare Pautasso. A conversation based approach for modeling REST APIs. In *12th Working IEEE/IFIP Conference on Software Architecture*, pages 165–174, 2015. DOI: 10.1109/WICSA.2015.20 25

Tom Heath and Christian Bizer. Linked data: Evolving the Web into a global data space. *Synthesis Lectures on the Semantic Web: Theory and Technology*, 1(1):1–136, 2011. DOI: 10.2200/s00334ed1v01y201102wbe001 xvii, 6

Ivan Herman, Ben Adida, Manu Sporny, and Mark Birbeck. RDFa 1.1 primer-rich structured data markup for web documents. *W3C Working Group Note*, World Wide Web Consortium, 2015. https://www.w3.org/TR/rdfa-primer 14

Rinke Hoekstra, Albert Meroño-Peñuela, Kathrin Dentler, Auke Rijpma, Richard Zijdeman, and Ivo Zandhuis. An ecosystem for linked humanities data. In *European Semantic Web Conference*, pages 425–440, Springer, 2016. DOI: 10.1007/978-3-319-47602-5_54 67

Rinke Hoekstra, Albert Meroño-Peñuela, Auke Rijpma, Richard Zijdeman, Ashkan Ashkpour, Kathrin Dentler, Ivo Zandhuis, and Laurens Rietveld. The dataLegend ecosystem for historical statistics. *Journal of Web Semantics*, 50:49–61, 2018. DOI: 10.1016/j.websem.2018.03.001 67

Aidan Hogan, Eva Blomqvist, Michael Cochez, Claudia d'Amato, Gerard de Melo, Claudio Gutierrez, José Emilio Labra Gayo, Sabrina Kirrane, Sebastian Neumaier, Axel Polleres, Roberto Navigli, Axel-Cyrille Ngonga Ngomo, Sabbir M. Rashid, Anisa Rula, Lukas Schmelzeisen, Juan Sequeda, Steffen Staab, and Antoine Zimmermann. Knowledge graphs, *Communications of the ACM*, 64(3), 2021. DOI: 10.1145/3418294 1, 2

Martynas Jusevičius. Linked data templates: Generic read-write linked data API. *Technical Report*, W3C Draft Community Group, 2020. 76

Ali Khalili and Klaas Andries de Graaf. Linked data reactor: Towards data-aware user interfaces. In *13th International Conference on Semantic Systems*, pages 168–172, 2017. DOI: 10.1145/3132218.3132231 76

Ali Khalili and Albert Meroño-Peñuela. WYSIWYQ-what you see is what you query. In *VOILA@ISWC*, pages 123–130, 2017. 68

Tobias Kuhn, Albert Meroño-Peñuela, Alexander Malic, Jorrit H. Poelen, Allen H. Hurlbert, Emilio Centeno Ortiz, Laura I. Furlong, Núria Queralt-Rosinach, Christine Chichester, Juan M. Banda, et al. Nanopublications: A growing resource of provenance-centric scientific linked data. In *IEEE 14th International Conference on e-Science (e-Science)*, pages 83–92, 2018. DOI: 10.1109/e-science.2018.00024 66

Pasquale Lisena and Raphaël Troncy. Transforming the JSON output of SPARQL queries for linked data clients. In *WWW'18 Companion: The Web Conference Companion*, Lyon, France, ACM, 2018. DOI: 10.1145/3184558.3188739 52

Pasquale Lisena, Albert Meroño-Peñuela, Tobias Kuhn, and Raphaël Troncy. Easy web API development with SPARQL transformer. In *18th International Semantic Web Conference (ISWC), In-Use Track*, pages 454–470, Auckland, New Zealand, 2019. DOI: 10.1007/978-3-030-30796-7_28 xvi, 52, 65, 71

Deborah L. McGuinness, Frank Van Harmelen, et al. OWL web ontology language overview. *W3C Recommendation*, 10(10), 2004. 3

Albert Meroño-Peñuela and Rinke Hoekstra. grlc makes GitHub taste like linked data APIs. In *European Semantic Web Conference*, pages 342–353. Springer, 2016. DOI: 10.1007/978-3-319-47602-5_48 xvi

Albert Meroño-Peñuela and Rinke Hoekstra. Automatic query-centric API for routine access to linked data. In *16th International Semantic Web Conference (ISEC)*, pages 334–349, Springer, 2017. DOI: 10.1007/978-3-319-68204-4_30 xvi, 65

Albert Meroño-Peñuela, Victor de Boer, Marieke van Erp, Willem Melder, Rick Mourits, Auke Rijpma, Ruben Schalk, and Richard Zijdeman. Ontologies in CLARIAH: Towards interoperability in history, language and media. *ArXiv Preprint ArXiv:2004.02845*, 2020. 65

Laurens Rietveld and Rinke Hoekstra. The YASGUI family of SPARQL clients. *Semantic Web*, 8(3):373–383, 2017. DOI: 10.3233/sw-150197 71

Guus Schreiber, Yves Raimond, Frank Manola, Eric Miller, and Brian McBride. RDF 1.1 primer. *W3C Recommendation*, World Wide Web Consortium, 2014. http://www.w3.org/TR/rdf11-primer/ 3, 6

Gurnoor Singh, Arnold Kuzniar, Matthijs Brouwer, Carlos Martinez-Ortiz, Christian W. B. Bachem, Yury M. Tikunov, Arnaud G. Bovy, Richard G. F. Visser, and Richard Finkers. Linked data platform for Solanaceae species. *Applied Sciences*, 10(19):2020. DOI: 10.3390/app10196813 66

Steve Speicher, John Arwe, and Ashok Malhotra. Linked data platform 1.0. *W3C Recommendation*, World Wide Web Consortium, 2015. http://www.w3.org/TR/2015/REC-ldp-20150226/ 2

Manu Sporny, Dave Longley, Gregg Kellogg, Markus Lanthaler, Pierre-Antoine Champin, and Niklas Lindström. SPARQL 1.1 Overview. W3C Recommendation, World Wide Web Consortium, 2013. https://www.w3.org/TR/json-ld11// xvi

Ruben Taelman, Joachim Van Herwegen, Miel Vander Sande, and Ruben Verborgh. Comunica: A modular SPARQL query engine for the Web. In *17th International Semantic Web Conference (ISWC)*, October 2018a. https://comunica.github.io/Article-ISWC2018-Resource/ DOI: 10.1007/978-3-030-00668-6_15 19

Ruben Taelman, Miel Vander Sande, and Ruben Verborgh. GraphQL-LD: Linked data querying with GraphQL. In *17th International Semantic Web Conference (ISWC), Poster and Demo Track*, Monterey, CA, 2018b. 22

Ruben Taelman, Miel Vander Sande, and Ruben Verborgh. Bridges between GraphQL and RDF. In *W3C Workshop on Web Standardization for Graph Data*, Berlin, Germany, 2019. 22

Peter van den Besselaar and Ali Khalili. Using the SMS data platform: RISIS deliverable 12. *Technical Report*, Vrije Universtiteit, 2018. 68

Willem Robert van Hage, with contributions from: Tomi Kauppinen, Benedikt Graeler, Christopher Davis, Jesper Hoeksema, Alan Ruttenberg, and Daniel Bahls. SPARQL: SPARQL client, 2013. http://CRAN.R-project.org/package=SPARQL R package version 1.15. 67

Pierre-Yves Vandenbussche, Ghislain A. Atemezing, María Poveda-Villalón, and Bernard Vatant. Linked open vocabularies (LOV): A gateway to reusable semantic vocabularies on the Web. *Semantic Web*, 8(3):437–452, 2017. DOI: 10.3233/sw-160213 2

Ruben Verborgh. Re-decentralizing the Web, for good this time. In Oshani Seneviratne and James Hendler, Eds., *Linking the World's Information: A Collection of Essays on the Work of Sir Tim Berners-Lee*, ACM, 2020. https://ruben.verborgh.org/articles/redecentralizing-the-web/ 19

Ruben Verborgh and Ruben Taelman. LDflex: A read/write linked data abstraction for front-end web developers. In *19th International Semantic Web Conference (ISWC)*, pages 193–211, Springer International Publishing, Athens, Greece, 2020. DOI: 10.1007/978-3-030-62466-8_13 19

Denny Vrandečić and Markus Krötzsch. Wikidata: A free collaborative knowledgebase. *Communications of the ACM*, 57(10):78–85, 2014. DOI: 10.1145/2629489 xv, 11

W3C SPARQL working group. SPARQL 1.1 overview. *W3C Recommendation*, World Wide Web Consortium, 2013. https://www.w3.org/TR/sparql11-overview/ xv, 7, 10, 11

K. E. D. Wapenaar. TNO early research program 2015–2018 annual report 2016. *Technical Report*, TNO, 2017. 68

Antony J. Williams, Lee Harland, Paul Groth, Stephen Pettifer, Christine Chichester, Egon L. Willighagen, Chris T. Evelo, Niklas Blomberg, Gerhard Ecker, Carole Goble, et al. Open PHACTS: Semantic interoperability for drug discovery. *Drug Discovery Today*, 17(21–22):1188–1198, 2012. DOI: 10.1016/j.drudis.2012.05.016 26

Authors' Biographies

ALBERT MEROÑO-PEÑUELA

Albert Meroño-Peñuela is a Lecturer (Assistant Professor) in Computer Science and Knowledge Engineering in the Department of Informatics of King's College London (United Kingdom). He obtained his Ph.D. at the Vrije Universiteit Amsterdam in 2016, under the supervision of Frank van Harmelen, Stefan Schlobach, and Andrea Scharnhorst. His research focuses on Knowledge Graphs, Web Querying, and Cultural AI. Albert has participated in large Knowledge Graph infrastructure projects in Europe, such as CLARIAH, DARIAH, and Polifonia H2020, and has published research in ISWC, ESWC, the *Semantic Web Journal*, and the *Journal of Web Semantics*. He is, together with Rinke Hoekstra, the original author of *grlc*, and together with Carlos Martínez-Ortiz, its main current maintainer.

PASQUALE LISENA

Pasquale Lisena is a researcher in the Data Science department at EURECOM, Sophia Antipolis (France). He obtained his Ph.D. in Computer Science from Sorbonne University of Paris in 2019, with a thesis on music representation and recommendation, under the supervision of Raphaël Troncy. His research focuses on Semantic Web, Knowledge Graphs, and Information Extraction, with particular application to the domain of Digital Humanities, contributing on AI projects such as DOREMUS, SILKNOW, and Odeuropa. Pasquale's work has been published in leading conferences in the field, such as ISWC, EKAW, and ISMIR. Given his past background as a web developer, his interest also involves data usability in web applications and human-computer interaction. He is the main author of *SPARQL Transformer*.

CARLOS MARTÍNEZ-ORTIZ

Carlos Martínez-Ortiz is a community manager at the Netherlands eScience Center. He obtained his Ph.D. in Computer Science at the University of Exeter (United Kingdom). Afterward, he worked on various research projects at the University of Exeter, Plymouth University, and the eScience Center. These projects were in collaboration with industrial and academic partners in diverse fields such as veterinary science, digital humanities, and life sciences. He has been involved in large projects such as CLARIAH and ODISSEI and works in close collaboration with partners such as SURF, DANS, and The Software Sustainability Institute. His current research interests include linked open data, natural language processing, and software sustainability.

Printed in the United States
by Baker & Taylor Publisher Services